Good Cop
Bad Cop

Eric Betts PhD

ISBN: 978-1-960853-25-7

Liberation's Publishing LLC
West Point - Mississippi

Contents

1 Introduction and Background

American society, since the time of the first settlements by the pilgrims, had hardly imagined the rise of any religious faith other than those founded upon a Eurocentric Christian worldview. The pilgrims came to the shores of America as asylum seekers from the conflicts and persecution which they suffered at the hands of the state churches which they left behind in Europe. They came to the New World where they could worship God freely according to the dictates of their own conscience and not that of the state. Nearly all of the presidents, governors, mayors, educators, and civil servants of American history were either bible-believers or persons who held it in the highest regard; most of the bible- believing officeholders were Christian in their backgrounds. It would be extremely difficult to find among America's early settlers those who would be champions of the Koran or other holy texts. Even in contemporary times it would be exceedingly rare to find high profile public figures that are Muslim, yet the door for such is open.

The experiences which the pilgrims suffered in the old world would later form the basis for the Constitution of the United States and the Bill of Rights. They wanted to ensure certain freedoms which were denied in the Old World. It was the idea of freedom of religion, which for the most part sprang forth within the realm of a Euro-Christian perspective, which made room for the later appearance of an obscure Muslim movement in America in the early twentieth century. This movement began among newly socially conscious blacks in the 1930s. They taught that the original and natural religion of black people was Islam and that this had been stolen from them during slavery by their oppressors. They declared that Christianity was the "white man's" religion imposed on them by their slave-masters to keep them ignorant and submissive.

It was the understanding of the Black Muslims that in order to return to their true African identity, and to be lifted up from their debased condition, they must rid themselves of the white man's Christianity and embrace Islam. It is a fact of history that Islam was present in West Africa during the time of the Trans-Atlantic Slave Trade and that the Moors who had traveled to the Americas in the pre-colonial times were Muslim. Despite this, Islam was little known within the American social structure from its earliest times until the first half of the twentieth century. Prior to the arrival of the Black Muslim, most blacks would have never envisioned that it was even possible to subscribe to any faith other than Christianity. Although most were illiterate, many talented black Christian preachers and orators arose in America's history. When the Black-Muslim orators arose, it was obvious that they were cut from a different cloth. The ideology of the Nation of Islam, founded largely by Elijah Muhammad, answered a particular yearning in the minds of Black Americans who had been long suffering under the weight of second-class citizenship. Many Christian preachers were fearful of speaking out against the social structure of the day, and most blacks of that period suffered from an unwitting self-hatred. This self-hatred had reached proportions which made many of them wish that they were not black and that they had been born white. As a result of the miseducation of African Americans, Africa was considered savage and a place to be despised. Their African heritage was a source of shame. When Elijah Muhammad launched his Muslim campaign in America, it would introduce a new and unorthodox version of Islam. It would represent a brand of Islam that would almost appear unrecognizable to the Muslims of Arabia and North Africa. It would be a unique creation of Islam which would address a particular need for self-pride among blacks in America who subconsciously viewed themselves as inferior to the larger society of Whites. Elijah Muhammad and his ministers would publicly address the power structure of the times in ways that most blacks were hesitant to speak about in private. When Elijah Muhammad began his "re-education" of Black people in America, this launched a dramatic shift in religious thought among black people and in the larger segment of American life. America has not been the same ever since.

The Black Muslim phenomenon has impacted not only religious life in America, but also athletics, politics, and popular culture. This religious order may be considered a social justice movement train on religious wheels. It is for this reason that they find large support and appreciation among non-adherents. The impact of this sect is felt among many Christian believers in the black community and in the larger civil rights movement. The Nation of Islam has even gained a respectful audience among non-blacks in America due to its outcry for justice and defense of the weak. The movement was a dynamic interruption to the centuries' long trend of political and religious thinking and its effects continue to be felt to this day.

C. Eric Lincoln is introduced in his volume (The Black Muslims in America) as one who served as a professor of religion and culture at Duke University. His book was hailed as "one of the best technical case studies in the whole literature of the social sciences."[1] His volume is considered by sociologists as the most comprehensive study on the black-Muslim movement in the United States. This classic sociological study gives a concise, accessible introduction to Islam, a movement born as an organized form of religious and social protest against a society sharply divided by race, for Americans whose knowledge of religion is limited primarily to Euro-Christianity. Alex Haley, who wrote The Autobiography of Malcolm X, was a contemporary of Lincoln. The two men often dialogued together as observers of the perplexities and impact of the black-Muslim movement. Both men illustrate in their work, the phenomena, the attraction, and society's reaction to its growth. Because the Nation of Islam outlived the assassination of Malcolm X, Lincoln's writing continued long after his death. Lincoln's work is much more expansive as he examined the sect more than the

---

[1] C. Eric Lincoln, *The Black Muslims in America*, third Edition (Grand Rapids Michigan: William B. Eerdmans, 1994), reviews.

individual personalities within the sect. Each is instructive as it relates to black religion, black protest and black consciousness today.

2 Sociological Causes of Nation of Islam's Early Growth

One of the areas of exploration in the field of social science is the cause of religion. What brought about the rise of the peculiar socio-religious group which came to be known as the Nation of Islam? What was the state of the world during the time of its rise? What were the conditions in society which triggered its formation? Even in today's cosmopolitan setting, the religion of Islam continues to be viewed as foreign system of worship which is not a part of the American tradition. Despite this, Islam continues to thrive in American society, mostly among black Americans. How did this come to be in a majority Christian nation where churchgoing is considered honorable and respectable? Lincoln goes into detail as he answers this question:

> All observers agree that its influence is already a significant factor in the black community and that it is increasing. The Muslim mosques, though reduced in number from the peak they reached in the early sixties, are well attended, and the ever-hustling ministers who serve Elijah Muhammad command the admiration and respect of many who accept Elijah but eschew his discipline. Just what are the Black Muslims after? And what are their chances of achieving it? To answer these questions, we shall have to look at the sociological drama of contemporary America, especially at the increasing dissatisfaction of African Americans with the bit role they have been permitted to play. As one Muslim minister put it in the early days of the

movement, 'We've just had a 'walk-on' part. We've been nothing but background scenery for everybody else. Now we've got something to say, and we are going to say it loud enough for the whole world to hear.' Could he have been foreshadowing the 'Say it real loud, I'm black and I'm proud' syndrome of the late sixties: Certainly, the Muslims played a major part in the development of black pride and black self-confidence[2]

It may come as a surprise to many who are somewhat familiar with the Nation of Islam that it was not the first Muslim organization to attract the attention of African Americans. The first Muslim group to gain the attention of the American public was the Moorish Science Temple founded by Noble Drew Ali. It is not by accident that much of the culture of the Nation of Islam may also be seen in the culture of the Moorish Science Temple. It is also not an accident that both of these groups gained their popularity in the northern cities of America. Noble Drew Ali drew his inspiration from Marcus Garvey, one of the early recognized leaders within the black community in the urban northern cities in the twentieth century. Garvey promoted Pan-Africanism, which is a political ideology which calls for the social unity of all blacks throughout Africa, America, South America and the Caribbean for the economic, educational, and political progress of the race. Garvey created a black national anthem, a flag for black unity, and other national emblems depicting a nation within a nation. His organization was

---

[2] C. Eric Lincoln, *The Black Muslims in America*, third Edition (Grand Rapids Michigan: William B. Eerdmans, 1994), 5.

called the Negro Improvement Association. This was mainly an educational association and social fraternity for the betterment of the people. It was also referred to as the "Back to Africa" movement. Garvey was later deported to his homeland of Jamaica for what many consider "trumped up" charges of mail fraud. Religion was not in the forefront of this movement, but as with most black American organizations' religion was indeed present. This movement gained the admiration and respect of tens of thousands of supporters throughout America. Members of the United Negro Improvement Association did not have to leave the church to become a member; they were not required to change their religion. Garvey never professed to be a prophet, savior, or divine messenger. His movement enjoyed most of its fame in the 1920s.

When Noble Drew Ali founded the Moorish Science Temple in Chicago, he adopted the Pan-African ideas of Garvey. He also embraced many of the disciplines such as uniform ways of dressing, culture, and emphasis on Garvey along with Muslim religious ideas at its foundation. He was the first in the post-reconstruction era to bring Muslim ideas into the public view as a black American, and the first to become popular doing so. Wallace Fard, who laid the groundwork for the development of the Nation of Islam, was influenced by Noble Drew Ali and his temple. The Nation of Islam today continues to mimic many of the cultural dynamics of Garvey's movement. Onetime devout member of Louis Farrakhan's re-established Nation of Islam, Vibert L. White Jr, who wrote extensively about his experience in the movement, says that "Elijah

Muhammad, a product of Marcus Garvey's Universal Negro Improvement Association, followed the ideas of (Booker T) Washington and continued promoting the theory of hard work, self-sufficiency, and black capitalism."[3]

Fard began his own Muslim group among African Americans after his break with the Moorish Science Temple, and shortly thereafter he would be discovered by Elijah Muhammad. Elijah Muhammad, who succeeded Fard shortly after the Nation of Islam began, was also an attendee at the Moorish Science Temple. The idea of "Moorish Science" was a concept introduced to promote pride in black identity in America after centuries of suffering from a corporate inferiority complex due to slavery and sharecropping. The Moors, they believed, were the ancestors of blacks in America. The idea was shared that the Moors were the most intelligent and accomplished in history and that the Moors had discovered America long before Columbus arrived. This re-education of blacks to redeem them from their inferiority complex was in the tradition of Garvey.

This was designed to illustrate how they can again become great and respected among other races. The concept of re-education of blacks for the purpose of pride and social development was carried forward in the public ministries of Fard and Elijah Muhammad. They, like Noble Drew Ali, would do so through the avenue of a black American version of Islam. They have ever been a subject of

---

[3] Vibert L. White, *Inside the Nation of Islam* (Gainesville: University Press of Florida, 2001), 62. A Historical Personal Testimony of a Black-Muslim

observation because as Lincoln put it, "The Black Muslims are probably America's foremost black nationalist movement"[4] They were able to convince hundreds that Islam was the original and natural religion of African Americans from a historical point of view. Robert Dannin, professor of linguistics and anthropology at Brown University, observes the following links between the enslaved in America, indigenous African Religions and the Islam.

> Beginning in the late seventeenth century a significant number of African Muslims were introduced into the Atlantic slave trade. Estimating on the basis of their ethnic origin, approximately 15 percent of the African slaves sold in North America came from nominally Muslim tribes...Islam figured as one amid a plurality of indigenous African religions that came to be mixed with elements of the slave-owners' Hebrew and Christian teachings.[5]

They alleged that this original religion was stolen from them during slavery. Interestingly enough, Fard was not a black man, but was thought to be either Turkish or White.

Even though the black-Muslims have from the beginning stressed the importance of unity within the black community, it has often been the case that internal divisions based on the politics of personality have created splintering among them. These occurrences reveal that one's own individual aspirations within a sect may often trump the overall goals of unity and ultimate victory. Vibert L White, shows why Elijah Muhammad was so closely identified with

---

[4] Lincoln, 2.
[5] Robert Dannin, *Black Pilgrimage to Islam* (New York: Oxford University Press, 2002), 16.

Fard and how this led to his rise.

> In 1932 Fard was arrested and imprisoned for the sacrificial
> death of John J. Smith. He was released but forced to leave
> Detroit. In 1933 Fard resurfaced in Chicago, where again he
> was arrested and imprisoned for various charges. Elijah
> Muhammad, a devout follower, offered Fard refuge in his
> home in Chicago. In early 1934 Fard Muhammad disappeared
> for the last time.[6]

It was under the leadership of Elijah Muhammad that the new
phase of black Muslim identity began to make its mark on society.
The fact that Fard had disappeared combined with his close
relationship with Elijah Muhammad generated the respect and
admiration he came to enjoy. The mysterious nature of Fard's
disappearance also made room for speculation concerning whether
he was a man of divine or supernatural origin. Elijah would use this
speculation to lend support for his leadership. Concerning Fard, one
writer details other areas of speculation that would follow his
departure. Vibert L. White provides valuable insider insights into
the various NOI versions of the history on what became of Fard and
Elijah's eventual rise.

> The official line of the Nation is that he left for Mecca.
> However, several members of the early Nation argued that he
> was befriended by individuals such as his student Elijah
> Muhammad and a former minister named Augustus
> Muhammad. These individuals suggest that Elijah ousted his
> teacher to become the new leader. Older insiders also suggest
> that Augustus constantly challenged Fard's ideals, ultimately
> believing that he was a better leader than Fard Muhammad.
> Augustus, holding this view, created a rival Muslim

---

[6] White, 31.

organization in 1933 called Development of our Own.[7]

During the first thirty years of the twentieth century, Jim Crow laws became the standard and norm of Southern society. These laws were invented to reverse the gains of blacks following the civil war and to create a two-tier citizenry. These laws protected those who were considered rightful citizens under the constitution, and stripped blacks of various constitutional rights. The penal code for blacks was exceedingly more punitive than the codes for their white counterparts. There was also a higher hurdle to exercise the right to vote for blacks than whites. These laws were designed to keep blacks in an inferior place for the preservation of the political, economic, and societal interests of white society. It must be remembered that immediately following the end of the civil war, while union troops remained in the South, former slaves voted and held office freely. It is almost unimaginable that in the years following the surrender of the Confederacy, Hiram Revels and Blanche K. Bruce (two black men,) were elected and served as U.S. senators. It would not be until the 1960s that another African American would serve in the U.S. Senate. Barack Obama, who later became president of the United States, was only the second black American to serve as a U.S. senator after the initial two men served following the Civil War. During the years following the implementation of reconstruction, literacy tests and unreasonable poll taxes were implemented to prevent blacks from voting or

---

[7] Ibid., 62.

holding office. Upon the election of Rutherford B. Hayes, and the consequent removal of Union troops from the former Confederacy, the knight riders began to terrorize Southern blacks with impunity. The Ku Klux Klan was accountable to no one; they were a secret society. There were also law-enforcement officials and judges who were members of the group. They threatened those black Americans who sought to exercise their constitutional rights or who were advancing too far beyond their "place." Extra-judicial lynching of blacks became an accepted norm.

Another institution was introduced during the years following reconstruction called "sharecropping." Many (if not most) former slaves immediately became sharecroppers for their former slave-masters. It was a system which allowed the former enslaved persons to live and work on the land in exchange for allowing the landowner to have the larger share of the crop which yielded. The tenants were allowed a smaller share of the crops to eat or sell on the market. The crops were considered rent. However, many of these slave-masters neglected to treat their tenants with equity and fairness. The landowner would often increase the cost of living and working on the land so that the tenants would be eternally indebted to him. Thus, they had to work from sunrise to sunset simply in order to meet the demands of the landowner and the family. This system would often require them to work without profit. It appeared as if the sharecropper system was simply a transition from one form of slavery to another. It should be remembered that these formerly enslaved people did not have the luxury or even the fortitude to sue their former slave-masters. Life-threatening consequences may follow such an action. This sharecropping system continued well beyond the first half of the twentieth century. Cotton continued as the major industry that it had always been during the time of legal slavery. Then former slaves and their descendants found ways to cope in a world of injustice and second-class citizenship.

The chief way of coping with suffering among the former slaves and their children was through religion. Christian religion was considered the primary answer to the plight which they were forced to endure. Islam was not a part of the fabric of religious idealism in the black south in the period following reconstruction. The "Great Migration" occurring in the Northern cities was also viewed as a means of escape as Ohio and Pennsylvania had been during slavery years. The Islamic religious identity would be introduced as a stronger reaction to their plight as millions began to arrive in the Northern and Midwestern cities of America. The rise of the Nation of Islam in America demonstrates what sociologists have long observed, which is how political and economic values impact religious views and sometimes vice versa. Richard Brent Turner is Professor in the Department of Religious Studies and the African American Studies Program at the University of Iowa; he observes the following connections to the black economics of the great migration and the rise of the black Muslims.

The basic social fact predisposing blacks to conversion to the Nation of Islam during this formative period was the Great Migration (1915-1930), during which great numbers of blacks left the South to find work in the cities of the North. The Great

Migration set the stage for the cultural exchanges between different groups of people and for black economic exploitation in the North, both of which help explain the dramatic changes in name and identity that occurred among the black Muslims...Their failure in the North was not their own personal failure but was due to large structural factors. Black workers became part of a new economic system in the North that profited from a supply of cheap labor that was both substitutable and disposable. Although the black migrants were a 'highly selective population,' there was no room for their upward mobility in this new system, in which they were forced to take and keep jobs that white people did not want. Ironically, their movement from the South and their exploitation in the North had been planned in the boardrooms of northern businesses in order to benefit 'American economic development."[8]

The great migration began with great promise and encouraging optimism but ended with hopelessness for the future of society. The Great Migration was helpful in creating an environment where blacks could better educate themselves and enjoy a certain level of independence not experienced during the sharecropping era. What it failed to achieve was equal citizenship, and it failed to end exploitation of the so-called lower classes. The Great Depression made matters even worse.

It was during this pilgrimage that many black Americans became open to new ideas as they began exercising their independence from slaveholders and landowners for the first time. It was in the industrial cities that they began to be introduced to black- Muslim

---

[8] Richard Brent Turner, *Islam in the African American Experience* (Indianapolis: Indiana University Press, 1997), 153.

philosophy. What was it that made it attractive? It addressed directly the injustice of their second-class status in society and introduced a new concept of pride in oneself. It taught against second class citizenship and reconnected its hearers to a glorious ancestral past in the Afro-Asian world. They regularly declared that Christianity was the "white man's" religion and that it was largely the institution responsible for their plight. They trumpeted the idea that Islam was the natural religion for Blacks and that it had been craftily stolen from them by their oppressors. This was believable because of the exploitation that they had witnessed during sharecropping years and the more recent exploitation by the company owners of the industrial North. Vibert L. White agrees with this assessment from an insider's viewpoint; he explains:

> [The Nation of Islam] a unique organization that combined social-religious programs that incorporated spirituality, conservative political ideologies, economic empowerment, and social uplift of the race. Their race activism caught the imagination of millions of black Americans who dedicated themselves to the ideology that formed the Black Muslims.[9]

What made the black-Muslims different than most civil justice organizations was the fact that they taught separation was more favorable to their plight than integration. Their only demand of the United States government was that they be granted one-fifth of the country's land for their own independent home. The Muslims argued that black- Americans would be a more powerful force in the world separated from whites and working united for the progress of

---

[9] White, 34.

the race. They taught that personal morals would prepare for the "promised land." C. Eric Lincoln explains how the aspirations of black Zionism appealed to so many hearts.

> Their ultimate demand—that blacks be allowed to set up a separate state within the United States occupying as much as one-fifth of the nation's territory—commands attention among non-Muslims, and the lashing indictment of whites that supports the demand strikes a responsive chord in many African American hearts.[10]

Should the government fail to grant them their just due, God himself would judge America, and that they would ultimately receive their demands. The concept that Whites were devils was also attractive, though it led to the sect being labeled as a hate organization by the larger society. Others view this form of hate as a response to being on the receiving end of generations of hate. Mike Wallace viewed this minority religious reaction to societal oppression in his 1950s black-Muslim documentary as The Hate that Hate Produced. They viewed the biblical "Hell" as the racism and discrimination which blacks suffered instead of the orthodox Christian way of understanding it. It is this very dynamic which led sociologists to declare that religion is often a reaction and counterbalance to the realities of historical developments in society. The black-Muslims themselves understood the sociological impact of their message of doom to America because of America's mal-treatment of blacks. According to Lincoln, such ideas were viewed as a means of asserting one's humanity against efforts to dehumanize

---

[10] Lincoln, 2.

them and to push back against the powerful who sought to exploit them; he says the following:

> Their message was well calculated to disturb even further a nation already unnerved by the traumas of the Great Depression. It was a blatant message of black assertion at a time of unprecedented anxiety for everyone, and most of all for the traditional power elite, who always interpret any suggestion of change as a threat. Those in control usually view the way things are as the way things ought to be. They view the status quo as the best of all possible arrangements, accepting their own good fortune as personal validation and viewing as deficient all who fall outside their peculiar circle of fortune. But the years out of which Black Muslims emerged pressed the status quo to the limit and beyond. It was an era in which the resilience of the human spirit in the face of adversity was tested in unprecedented ways.[11]

While the larger majority population along with black Americans were charging the Elijah Muhammad sect with being a hate group, his followers' counterargument was that Blacks already hated themselves as a result of White oppression and the negative stereotype of ancestral Africa. They argued that their social and religious expression was not hate but an effort to re-educate black Americans to love their own kind and to cure them of their generations-long inferiority complex. Lincoln further expounds upon this dynamic and states the following:

> Although the Nation of Islam was as distinctive in its peculiar bid for the reins of history as any of the other socio-religious expressions mentioned above, it was nonetheless a part of the unending effort to redress the excesses or the insufficiencies of a past unreconciled to a self-perceived

---

[11] Ibid., xx.

identity. Such movements are usually of limited duration or impact. They tend either to implode under the weight of their deficits or linger on as mere symbols after having been eclipsed by failure or by some more attractive alternative that addresses the same concerns. But the Black Muslims, the Nation of Islam remain a feature of contemporary life after more than sixty years, and they continue to have a remarkable impact on the concerns, the thinking, and the behavior of large numbers of the American people.[12]

The most popular black-Muslim in contemporary times (next to Muhammad Ali) is the late Malcolm X. He is attributed with bringing the black-Muslim movement into the American limelight. Prior to the rise of Malcolm X, only a tiny percentage of whites had ever heard of the group. Malcolm was considered extremely intelligent, eloquent, sharp, quick-witted, and telegenic. Elijah Muhammad was not known to be a great speaker and had a very frail appearance. He lacked the energy and enthusiasm of the younger Malcolm. Unlike Muhammad, Malcolm had the ability to connect with a larger non-Muslim audience of blacks in the form of social protest. He came into prominence at the beginning of the television age of the late 50s and early 60s. He is almost single- handedly responsible for the significant growth of their temples and membership during this period. The news media was drawn to him; he would explain to the world the "teachings of the honorable Elijah Muhammad." One writer, in referring to Malcolm's role in building up the Nation of Islam, stated, "When he resumed active leadership of the black Muslims in the late 1940s, there were four temples in

---

[12] Ibid., xxii.

the United States—in Chicago, Detroit, Milwaukee, and Washington, D.C."[13]

Alex Haley in his interview with Malcolm stated the following:

Malcolm X said that he had increased the Nation of Islam membership from about 400 when he had joined to around to around 40,000. 'I don't think there were more than 400 in the country when I joined. I really don't. They were mostly older people, and many of them couldn't even pronounce Mr. Muhammad's name, and he stayed mostly in the background.[14]

The aftermath of World War II was also a significant contributor to the rise of black-Muslim ideology in America. Black soldiers had contributed to their country in ways that had not been seen since serving in the Union army. No doubt, these black veterans were very proud of their contribution to society. Another question one may have asked, "If the black population is capable of fighting for their country, why should they not be able to fight for their own rights within American society?" Others may have asked, "If the black soldier has fought so bravely and sacrificially for his country, then why should he come home and be treated as a second-class citizen?" The end of World War II gave the black-Muslim movement even greater oxygen, which was followed by the rise of Malcolm X who brought the Nation of Islam into the National spotlight in the 50s and 60s. The aftermath of World War II, the coming era of black

---

[13] Turner, 153.

[14] Alex Haley, *The Autobiography of Malcolm X* (New York: Ballentine Books, 1965), 472.

protest, the strain of the black ghetto, the end of African colonialism and the public work of Malcolm X all intersected at the same time. This was all gasoline in the fire that would perhaps contribute to the Nation of Islam's greatest days. While the rise of Malcolm X greatly benefited the Nation of Islam, the dynamic of competition for leadership would later ensue. Haley states the following:

> During the 1950s, the Nation of Islam expanded its operations throughout the United States—dramatically increasing its membership and becoming the major voice for Islam in America. These changes occurred in the aftermath of World War II, as African Americans made their first 'decisive cracks in the citadel of white supremacy' and laid the groundwork for the black revolution of the 1950s and 1960s... Also in the 1940s, a second great wave of millions of Southern blacks began to enter the so-called 'Promised Land' of the Northern cities in the United States. This demographic factor is important because it brought to the Northern ghettos people who would become major actors in American Islam and the black protest movement in the 1960s.[15]

Malcolm X made an enormous contribution for the growth of the Muslim movement and for its public relations, yet his fame would later lead to a public break with Elijah Muhammad. An internal rivalry began to arise between the two leaders. In 1963, Malcolm X made intemperate remarks about the assassination of President Kennedy. Elijah Muhammad would later discipline and excommunicate Malcolm for being a preacher of violence, and Malcolm would later charge Elijah Muhammad with being a serial

---

[15] Richard Brent Turner, *Islam in the African American Experience* (Indianapolis: Indiana University Press, 1997), 169.

adulterer for impregnating his secretaries. It appeared as if Elijah Muhammad would rather have a Nation of Islam of smaller dimensions and below the public view, rather than being brought into a prominent position through the efforts of Malcolm. Sympathizers of Elijah Muhammad would later assassinated Malcolm because of the perceived threat he might pose to the movement and his charges against their "messenger." Alex Haley enlightens us concerning the trouble that was brewing within the movement in the following observation:

> And during those days, Dr. C. Eric Lincoln and I would talk on the phone fairly often. We rarely would fail to mention how it seemed almost certain that seeds of trouble lay in the fact that however much Malcolm X praised Elijah Muhammad, it was upon dramatic, articulate Malcolm X that the communications media and hence the general public focused the great bulk of their attention.[16]

Some would argue that the development and growth of the Nation of Islam was an extreme attempt on the part of black Americans to adjust to the pressures of discrimination in America. It was a way to openly express themselves about their true feelings about their status in America with the righteous cover of religion. The comfort zone of group identity was a major contributor as well; it is easier to stand against the system with the mutually aggrieved than standing alone. Nonetheless the Nation of Islam of the 1960s was viewed as a threat to social order and as anti-white establishment. This was thought to be a terrible stigma by the larger

---

[16] Haley, 467.

society. These perceptions were not denied by black-Muslims who did not view this surmising as necessarily a negative image. They saw themselves as resisting a greater evil and expressing the only legitimate reaction to their own anxieties concerning society. They did not mind the criticism of not being an orthodox version of Islam. They viewed their unique version as the only one that could address their specific needs and the ills that they faced. Robert Brent Turner addresses the sociological observations of C. Eric Lincoln, which he identifies as classical American sociological literature and offers his own critique.

(Lincoln was considered a friend and ally of NOI). His book is still the classic study of the Nation of Islam and a classic in sociological literature. But Lincoln, who was a sociologist of religion, formulated his own social-scientific signification of the Nation of Islam that echoed some of the images of the movement that had already been created by the white establishment. Lincoln's signification focused on the establishment of the Nation of Islam as a logical consequence of what he perceived as the pathology of urban, lower-class, black nationalism. Lincoln coined the term 'Black Muslims' to differentiate followers of the Nation of Islam from orthodox Muslims, whom he called 'moslems.' He advanced the theory that black Islam was primarily a social protest movement rooted in the anxiety and discontent of black lower-class migrants in the northern industrial cities.[17]

Certainly, the black Christian preachers and churches were on the front lines advocating for the advancement of their race during the time of the black-Muslim's rise. This also attracted many youths and even children to participate in the Civil Rights Movement. Despite

---

[17] Turner, 199.

this, Black Muslim leaders often charged Christian leaders with being pawns in the hands of the white world and ineffective. The Nation of Islam also attracted youth, many of whom were seeking to reform their lives after engaging in criminal activity, yet they were mostly on the sidelines while others actively fought for equal rights. Many, like Malcolm X, were converted to Islam while in prison. The youth that the Civil Rights Movement attracted were southern and rural, while the youth attracted to the Muslim movement were urban and victims of the ghetto. Other than the historical view of Christianity as the white-man's religion, there are the other factors which attract black youth to the Nation of Islam instead of the church. Cultural factors and religious traditions influenced by society may have been a factor, and Lincoln explains this phenomenon in the following terms:

The challenge of an ascetic ideal, balanced by the absence of social barriers to affiliation and service, has brought thousands under the banner of Muhammad. Probably in no other religious organization are alcoholics, ex-convicts, pimps, prostitutes, and narcotic addicts welcomed so sincerely. The Christian church is, in most instances, careful to take none to its bosom until they are cleansed.

As Lincoln sees it, the black Muslims have an unrivaled level of appeal to those who are considered the black underclass. Those who would otherwise be rejected by the black Middle Class are welcomed and embraced in the Nation of Islam.

3 The Three Sociological Attitudes

C. Eric Lincoln presents three possible sociological reactions by the abused minority toward those who abuse them. These, according to Lincoln, are all natural responses of any group of people who face unjust pressures by the larger society. He connects these responses to the reasons for the rise of the black-Muslims. He presents these responses as being as consequential and natural as the law of gravity. To understand these sociological responses, the observations of C. Eric Lincoln are instructive:

> There are] three types of response to pressure and discrimination: avoidance, acceptance, and aggression. These represent the attempts on the part of individuals to adjust to social hostilities directed against them. These same channels of response may also find a corporate expression. People organize in the face of a persistent threat. Plantation 'folk Negroes' are adjusting to social hostility when they go out alone to steal the white boss's corn or potatoes on Saturday night. They are no less adjusting when they lose themselves 'beyond Jordan' in company with their neighbors on Sunday morning. One response is a personal expression of resentment and counter aggression; the other is corporate escape. Each kind of response, personal and corporate, has its special advantages in relation to the situation that excites it.[18]

Examples of avoidance, according to Lincoln, are reflected in

---

[18] Lincoln, 231.

blacks avoiding white neighborhoods, businesses, and churches in order to avoid possible disrespect or even misunderstandings. Lincoln's example of acceptance is illustrated in the attitude of going along with and acting as if one accepts disrespect and abuse without protest. One extreme and complete example of avoidance in the black community was when in order to escape the consequences of their *"group identification [they] withdraw entirely by 'passing' into the dominant group."*[19] There are many examples in history of 'passing' into white society by light complexioned blacks who could be mistaken for white.

Lincoln points out that the larger society misinterprets "acceptance" as appreciation or resignation to the conditions. Haley observed an experience with Malcolm X who cited another writer. "He scribbled one night, 'You have not converted a man because you have silenced him. John Viscount Morley.'"[20]

The statement summed up how acceptance is often misinterpreted.

Lincoln also explains that the "aggression" mindset of a group represents active protest against perceived wrongdoing against one's minority group; sometimes this aggression is extreme. Lincoln finds that in some cases the mindset of group "aggression" may backfire as a result of possible overreaction in the law-enforcement and legal arena against such attitudes. Based on the analysis of Lincoln, the black-Muslim movement embraces the societal reaction

---

[19] Ibid, 231.
[20] Haley, 467.

of avoidance. They believed in conducting business among themselves and living in communities of black people. They promoted the idea of supporting black-owned businesses as better than patronizing their white counterparts. They did not believe in segregation or integration but embraced the peculiar idea of separation and independence from the white world. This is perhaps why they advocated for their own land to organize their own government within the United States territories. To a limited degree they also embraced "acceptance," because they believed in following the laws of the land without protest, even unjust laws. This manner of thinking is in agreement with sociologist Talcott Parson's idea that religion motivates society to behave morally and harmoniously and tends not to work for the overthrow of governments. Lincoln further clarifies this point in the following words:

> The Black Muslims are neither pacifists nor aggressors. They pay zealous attention to the requirements of the letter of the law regarding peace and order. They engage in no sit-ins, test no segregation statutes, participate in no marches on Washington or anywhere else. But they do believe in keeping scores even, and they have warned all America that "an eye for an eye and a tooth for a tooth is the only effective way to settle racial differences.[21]

The primary attitude that is most often attributed to the black-Muslim faith is that of aggression, because of their vocal attacks on white society and the U.S. government, their demand for their own

---

[21] Lincoln, 231.

land and country and their call for separation rather than integration. Lincoln defines this attribute of aggression in the following terms:

> Aggression—an act or pattern of behavior that aims to discomfort, injure, or destroy people or their values. Mounting boycotts, engaging in willful inefficiency or providing sloppy work for white employers refusing to observe the customary forms of etiquette—all these are direct means of expressing personal hostility...And of course aggression can also be vented in physical attacks. Literature, art, and humor are readily available vehicles of direct aggression, and they are widely used as such...Even responsible and controlled aggression as a response to offenses against one's human dignity is a dangerous undertaking, and it is shrouded in moral and ethical ambivalence. Many individuals prefer the paths of avoidance and acceptance.[22]

Black American leaders who employed political aggression against the system of second-class citizenship were often associated by government officials and politicians as being associated with America's enemies. Marcus Garvey, Elijah Muhammad, Malcolm X, Martin Luther King, and the NAACP were often accused of being agents of the Russians during the 60s or the Japanese in the 40s. Their challenge to the American system was looked upon as an attempt by foreign powers to unsettle national order. Civil Rights leaders were viewed as foreign pawns to thus weaken and embarrass the U.S. before the world. Such charges were unfounded and perhaps this was understood by those who made those claims. Although the Russians and Chinese would point to the hypocrisy of the United States in their treatment of minorities, this may not have

---

[22] Ibid, 37-38

been the root cause of such charges. What was the psychology behind such claims? Lincoln answers this question.

> Aggressive leaders will arise, however. Since they threaten the protective fantasy, the most militant of them must be discounted and isolated from the masses. By dismissing them as 'communists' or 'radicals' (or whatever is beyond the pale at any given moment), we can keep our fantasy of the contented African American pure.[23]

It should not be assumed that the black-Muslims were the only religious group which showcased the aggression response. Most of the challenges and changes to the second-class citizen trap came as the result of aggression responses of the black church during the Civil Rights Movement of the 1960s. The recruitment for the NAACP occurred within the church. Most of the marches and sit-in protests took place as a result of the church. Martin Luther King was criticized for his direct-action program in Birmingham Alabama by his fellow clergymen. It was for this reason that King penned the famous letter from the Birmingham jail. Many supporters of the civil rights movement supported a concept of gradualism, which advocated for patience as laws were slowly changing over time. The thinking was that society, and its laws were changing slowly and that black leaders should not interfere with the natural process through public protests against the system. Many felt that direct action campaigns would do more harm than good. Nat Turner, one of the most famous leaders of slave rebellions in the United States

---

[23] Ibid, 39.

was a Christian preacher and "prophet." Is there a higher level of aggression response than that of Nat Turner? Fredrick Douglass' campaigns for equality were based on Christian ideals; he often cited scripture in his speeches and carried a bible with him. Richard Allen's break with the main Methodist denomination to form the African Methodist Episcopal church is an example of the aggression response; he was protesting the unchristian racial practices in the church. Before Dr. King arrived as pastor of the Dexter Avenue Church in Montgomery, there was the more radical protest pastor of that church in the person of Reverend Vernon Johns. So why was the formation of a Muslim alternative possible or even necessary? Lincoln draws the following conclusion.

> Because Christianity is 'the white man's religion,' the repudiation of Christianity is an overt act of aggression against the whites. To be identified with a movement that openly rejects the fundamental values of the powerful majority is to increase vastly one's self-esteem and one's stature among peers. This social incentive to defiance is not limited to the Muslims; among the black intellectuals generally, a deviation from the Whites' way of doing things has come to be called 'independent thinking' and reaps its rewards...but the intellectuals remain within the orbit of white culture while the Muslims set themselves completely adrift.[24]

This concept is strangely akin to the Karl Marx viewpoint which declares that people are taken advantage of by the elite, and religion is the opiate of life. In the case of the black-Muslims, Christianity was the culprit, and Islam was the answer. In Marx's case, atheism

---

[24] Ibid, 27-28

was the answer. What Marx opposed was the idea that if you do as you are told and don't question then your reward will be in the afterlife. He felt that religion was a tool to keep the poor people in place and interfering with the unjust actions of the powerful few. Marx developed a low view of religion because of the church's use of political power. What Marx felt about religion generally was what Elijah Muhammad and his followers believed about Christianity. They saw Christianity as demanding that blacks stay in their place and their reward would be in heaven. The Christian religion as they viewed it, taught that blacks should be humble and submissive despite their terrible plight. Christian ministers, slave-masters, and white overlords would cite the bible and declare that servants should patiently obey their masters and not resist their authority. Black Muslim ideology was a complete rejection of this idea. Their philosophy agreed with Marx that Christianity was an opiate to keep the oppressed people in submission for their own economic and political exploitation. Unlike Marx, they view Islam as an intellectual awakening in that regard.

Lincoln suggests that such attitudes would not exist within aggrieved segments of society if it were not for the outside pressures which create those attitudes, and that group identification springs from those pressures. Many who joined groups such as the Nation of Islam were willing to overlook what they viewed as theological extremes and superstitions in exchange for the spirit of brotherhood and racial solidarity. Vibert L. White utilizes his history within the movement to explain the psychological need of most black people for solidarity and belonging, and how the "Nation" fulfills this hunger when he says the following:

> My indoctrination into the Nation was an exciting time. Even though there were blatant signs of racism, bigotry, and plain theological hogwash, I became increasingly committed to the overall theme of racial solidarity and the self-help principles espoused by the Nation.[25]

In some respects, it may be said that American society created the phenomenon known as the black Muslims. Lincoln explains the origin of minorities and group identification.

> Minorities are created by pressures exerted by the majority. If the majority did not choose to exclude a group, the group would not be a minority; it would be an indistinguishable part of the whole social body. In the same way, the sense of unity and cohesion that we call group identification develops in response to outside pressures. It is a way of ensuring not identity (the majority has seen to that) but the survival of the member and their most cherished values...Arnold and Caroline Rose have suggested that 'group identification is the minority's major defense against discrimination and prejudice from the majority.' This major defense seems to be clearly effective. Wherever people have exhibited a corporate unity in the face of social oppression, they have secured respect and often an abatement of persecution.[26]

Lincoln argued that societal pressures contributed to the rise of the Nation of Islam, yet the majority population in America was indeed shocked when Mike Wallace introduced the cult of Elijah Muhammad to the larger public. Wallace even chided "sober

---

[25] White, 60.
[26] Lincoln, 231.

minded" blacks for their silence concerning such a group in his introductory remarks to his documentary. What Wallace and the viewing audience may not have recognized is that the expressions by the black Muslims of condemnation against society at large, found a sympathetic ear among black Christians. Those Muslims such as Malcolm X openly declared what the Christian community would only express in private settings.

Nonetheless, the Muslims would mostly keep their thoughts among their own people and shied away from the public eye. One contemporary writer stated, "Perhaps it can be said that today's NOI, like the NOI of the 1930s and 1940s, operates largely outside of the consciousness of many Americans."[27]According to Wallace in his documentary, the Muslims were not interested in being televised, and almost turned him down. In fact, the only way he was able to video the first televised black-Muslim gathering, was that Louis Lomax was a black American and therefore allowed entrance into the event.

> In 1959 Mike Wallace and Louis Lomax created a television documentary on the organization titled 'The Hate that Hate Produced.' The program exhibited the Nation to the larger white American community for the first time. The white population saw a defiant, militant, anti-white religious organization of blacks who believed in total racial segregation. The Nation's doctrine to white Americans and many blacks was quite interesting and disturbing. [This was quite different from] the high-profile civil rights movement

---

[27] Edward E. Curtis, *Black Muslim Religion in the Nation of Islam* (Chapel Hill, North Carolina: University Of North Carolina Press, 2006), 185.

that called for social and political integration.[28]

Although many Americans were apprehensive about the political involvement of the Civil Rights movement of the 1950s and 60s, they were absolutely horrified by the public expressions and demands of the smaller black-Muslim Movement. It must be pointed out that the black-Muslims in the early days of its fame was publicly against the Civil Rights Movement and denounced its leadership. Their belief system forbade them to be involved in any matters of a political nature. This idea ran contrary to the heart of black protest in America and may represent the strongest downside of black-Muslim ideology. Only recently in contemporary times are Nation of Islam members becoming more politically active, yet their stigma of being pro-black but anti-political continues in the black community. Vibert L. White explains this anti-political and out of touch strain that runs throughout the movement.

> ...the Nation appeared out of touch with the mood of most African Americans. The Nation of Islam in the 1950s represented only a small fraction of the black community who favored separation over integration. Louis Farrakhan's Nation of the 1980s and 1990s would also run contrary to black mainstream thought. Farrakhan's view that there was an elaborate conspiracy by Jews and the United States government to destroy black Americans.[29]

One of the reactions to aggressive leadership responses is to overestimate the significance or impact of the leader. Some question

---

[28] White, 40-41
[29] Ibid, 40-41

whether the aggressive leader can be destructive of American ideals within the minds of the minority group. Others wonder whether the leader will give America a metaphorical "black eye" as contacts and communication are interchanged in the international arena. There are also those who fear the influence domestically of the leader who has behaved in a way that is perceived to be disloyal to America. Such leaders are feared because the public is concerned about possible disruptions to the peace among the races in America. The question that must then be asked is "are these fears unfounded?" America's response to Farrakhan's globe travelling may very well be an unnecessary overreaction. Vibert L. White observes the following:

> The Nation of Islam promotes Farrakhan as a global religious advocate who commands the attention of kings, presidents, dictators, and religious leaders. The American public, black and white, tend to believe this view. But close scrutiny reveals that Farrakhan's international fame is more myth than fact. Except for a few leaders like Qadhafi of Libya, very few world leaders take Farrakhan seriously. Thus, he is not an international black icon but a world traveler with a thirst for power, fame, and fortune.[30]

While Farrakhan may be respected by black Americans in the American homeland for reasons unique to their experience, this is not necessarily the case in the international arena. In fact, Farrakhan may have done more to harm his image abroad than to help. In some cases, he is viewed with disdain for his support of dictators who oppress their minorities while claiming to be a champion of the

---

[30] White, 187.

downtrodden. In some cases, while being viewed in America as a voice for the voiceless, in some places in the world he is viewed as an unwitting supporter of modern-day slavery. White agrees with this observation in the following words:

> [1995-1997] "...outside the presidential office of the Sudan, no one really paid attention to Farrakhan. He is known by the Muslim leadership, white and black Nubian Christians who regard him as an enemy. The Nubians do not understand why Farrakhan embraces Arabs, who are responsible for their enslavement, instead of supporting the fight of black Africans who share a heritage with African Americans.[31]

Sometimes leaders who advance an aggression response may also overestimate their own influence and abilities. It is for this reason that such leaders have made serious missteps in the advocacy of their cause. While Malcolm X is viewed as a great historical figure and pan-African icon among African countries, Farrakhan has attempted to replicate that experience. Those efforts have not always met with success in his case. The African public views Farrakhan from a different perspective than the black American public. White references the famous encounter of Farrakhan with Nelson Mandela and illustrates how he is viewed among African leaders. While he is indeed well known, his reputation has not always been viewed in a positive light. Vibert L White makes the following observation surrounding the exchange:

> Mandela was disturbed that Farrakhan entered South Africa with a twenty-two-member entourage and an

---

[31] White, 198.

aristocratic lifestyle that would have made any twentieth-century king jealous…During his stay Farrakhan had the fortune, or perhaps misfortune, of talking with President Mandela. Mandela severely reprimanded the minister for statements he had made calling Jews and whites devils, evil, and genetically inferior. Even though his government suffered from apartheid, stated Mandela, racism, discrimination, and racial baiting would not be tolerated in South Africa.[32]

Although this exchange occurred on an international stage, Farrakhan continued to maintain his prestige within the African American community back home. It was understood that most foreign leaders, including African ones, do not fully comprehend the plight of black people in America, and its support of leaders who advocate for them.

---

[32] Ibid, 199.

4 The Nation of Islam and Popular Culture

Another sociological aspect to consider is the relationship between the Nation of Islam and popular culture. In its early days the Nation of Islam taught their adherents about the evils of entertainment, sports, and boxing. Edward E. Curtis IV, professor of religious and Africana studies at the Indiana University School of Liberal Arts observes the following:

> Like other black religious groups formed during the first half of the twentieth century, the NOI condemned various aspects of black popular culture that it associated with the moral decline of the black body, including the polishing of nails, straightening of hair, gambling, and the wearing of short dresses. Black Muslims instead advocated 'clean living,' like many of their black brothers and sisters who were members of the Church of God in Christ, a black Pentecostal denomination, and other religious communities in which African Americans took part. The NOI also eschewed pork, as did many black Jews.[33]

However, this all changed when the Nation of Islam encountered the boxer who was at that time named Cassius Clay. He became the heavyweight champion in boxing and the most famous athlete ever in the history of sports. He was recruited heavily by Malcolm X, who thought that his efforts would restore him back into good

---

[33] Curtis, 97.

standing with the Nation. At this time, Malcolm had been silenced by Elijah Muhammad for remarks which he made about Kennedy's assassination as a matter of "chickens coming home to roost."[34] Malcolm X, after his period of censure stated that the "chickens coming home to roost" remark was not a celebration of the assassination, but a metaphor for the sure result of a sociological dynamic of an unrestrained "climate of hate."[35] The climate of ruthless killing of blacks would not stop at the color line and that the hatred would spread into other areas. This would be the cause of Kennedy's death, according to Malcolm. Malcolm's explanations of his past remarks did little to endear him to his mentor. His recruitment of Clay would not gain him any favor within the movement.

Under the leadership of Elijah Muhammad, Clay's name was changed to Muhammad Ali. During the early days of the Nation, all members bore the last name of "X." The "X" represented their unknown ancestral last name which was taken from them under slavery, and that God would one day in the future when all things are fulfilled grant them each a special last name. Only Elijah Muhammad had a last name, but a special exception would be made for Cassius Clay. The leadership would go against its own theology to make an exception for Clay due to the colossal role he played within American popular culture. This would perhaps never have

---

[34] Malcolm X. "*God's Judgment of White America*" (press conference, New York, December 1, 1963).
[35] Malcolm X, interview following the conversion of Cassius Clay to Muhammad Ali Lewis Lomax, New York, February 1, 1964.

happened had it not been for the fact of Clay's significance as a famous boxer. Clay's conversion to Muhammad Ali was received with a sense of pride among the adherents of Elijah Muhammad that he was one of their very own. Alex Haley commented on this history and interaction between Malcolm X and Cassius Clay in the following words:

> 'Malcolm X said that I should look forward now to Clay's quick development into a major world figure, I don't know if you really realize the world significance that this is the first Muslim champion.' ...It was the following morning when Cassius Clay gave the press interview which resulted in national headlines that he was actually a 'Black Muslim,' and soon after, the newspapers were carrying pictures of Malcolm X introducing the heavyweight champion to various African diplomats in the lobbies of the United Nations headquarters in New York City. Malcolm X toured Clay about in Harlem, and in other places, functioning, he said, as Clay's 'friend and religious advisor.[36]

In this scenario, we find popular culture changing the attitude of a religion. We also see popular culture changing the viewpoint of the public about the Nation of Islam. As consequence of this embrace by a leading figure of popular culture, the Nation of Islam is now viewed by the larger public as uniquely American rather than a foreign religion. The black Muslims would later have its impact on popular culture as famous basketball players would profess the Muslim religion. It is also interesting to note that while Muhammad Ali was vilified for his rhetoric and protest against the Vietnam War during the 60s, he died in 2016 under the admiration of presidents,

---

[36] Haley, 469.

senators and world leaders. President Bill Clinton gave the eulogy at his funeral. Was it because society changed, because Muhammad Ali changed, or both?

Lew Alcindor, the famous college basketball player from UCLA, would become Kareem Abdul-Jabbar who became even more famous as he played for the Milwaukee Bucks and Los Angeles Lakers. In the 1990s, there was Mike Tyson, the now infamous boxer, who also embraced the black-Muslim religion. It was not considered a strange thing when Hakeem Olajuwon openly professed his Muslim faith due to this acceptance within popular culture. In contemporary times there is a close connection and open admiration among popular singers and figures in the rap industry toward the work of Louis Farrakhan. Spike Lee's movie production entitled "Malcolm X," shined a significant light on the activism of the most popular black-Muslim and became a major hit in the film industry. Young people were wearing baseball caps with "X" emblazoned on them; it was a major fad. Imagery of Malcolm as a defiant and rebel-type figure was proudly worn on t-shirts. This was also an economic plus for those in the clothing industry; tens of millions of dollars were profited. However, the film was not well received among Nation of Islam adherents. Vibert L. White explains why the film disappointed NOI adherents:

> The film capitalized on a cultural nationalist rebirth of Malcolm among African American youth. In 1993 and 1994 the American youth later to be known as 'Generation X' became fascinated with the image of Malcolm as a bold, strong, and defiant black leader. As the image of Malcolm X grew among media personnel, Farrakhan's image and that of

the NOI diminished. Lee branded Elijah Muhammad and the Muslim inner circle as the group who murdered the Black Muslim leader.[37]

White also brings to view Farrakhan's status within the intersection of politics and popular culture. He adds, "Because the majority of black Americans saw Farrakhan as a major political leader who should be heard by the larger white majority, the minister enjoyed invitations from the talk-show hosts like Phil Donahue, Barbara Walters, and Arsenio Hall."[38]

---

[37] White, 116-117
[38] Ibid, 122.

5 The Peculiar Beliefs and Disciplines of the Nation of Islam

The beliefs and religious disciplines of the black-Muslims, which Fard likely borrowed from Noble Drew Ali, was expanded upon by the books written by Elijah Muhammad. They were later outlined in the official newspaper of the organization called *"Muhammad Speaks."* Unbeknownst to many, Louis Farrakhan is not the immediate successor of Elijah Muhammad. When Elijah Muhammad died in 1975, his son, Wallace Muhammad was named his successor. Farrakhan was initially a minister in the Nation of Islam who submitted to the leadership of Wallace Muhammad during his first few years as leader of the sect. Farrakhan is actually the leader of a revived Nation of Islam which would be more in harmony with Elijah Muhammad's teachings, while Wallace Muhammad moved the black-Muslims more in the direction of orthodox Islam. What Wallace Muhammad single-handedly achieved is monumental and unprecedented in the history of American religion. Curtis elaborates on the connection between Wallace Muhammad and earlier NOI mythology:

> Wallace Muhammad succeeded in altering the religious ideology of the movement without losing all of his followers. In a few years, he convinced thousands of African Americans to change the way they thought about and practiced aspects of Islam. In so doing, it must be recognized, he was working with persons who already

thought of themselves as Muslims…and that style of being Muslim endured the break with Elijah Muhammad's unique mythologies.[39]

Wallace Muhammad's leadership of the black-Muslim movement into the arena of orthodox Islam had its roots in the footsteps of Malcolm X in his final journey to Mecca during the last year of his life. Malcolm returned from Mecca and founded the Muslim Mosque Inc., located in New York, which was designed to teach black-Muslims how to become orthodox Muslims. Upon Malcolm's return from Mecca, he rejected the philosophy of his former mentor concerning the relationship between the races. No longer did he consider white society as generally devilish, but as a part of the brotherhood of mankind. Malcolm embraced whites as brothers but continued to advocate for the progress of the black race and also for the rights of blacks to bear arms for self-defense against their violent attackers. He was interviewed by several news organizations immediately upon his return. They asked him the following as recorded by Haley:

'Do we correctly understand that you now do not think that all whites are evil?' 'True, sir! My trip to Mecca has opened my eyes. I no longer subscribe to racism. I have adjusted my thinking to the point where I believe that whites are human beings…as long as this is borne out by their humane attitude toward Negroes…I'm not condemning whites for being whites, but for their deeds.'[40]

Remarkably, Malcolm began to embrace a concept that would be

---

[39] Curtis, 184.
[40] Haley, 475.

considered absolutely heretical to the principles of black-Muslim ideology; he was open to the idea of interracial marriage. This was an uncommon feature in American society during the lifetime of Civil Rights activism. The teachings of Elijah Muhammad advanced the idea of separation among the races from a social and geographical standpoint and interracial marriage was outside of the realm of possibilities. Now that he was free from the oversight of Elijah Muhammad, Malcolm had the freedom to criticize his former views and to think for himself. He advanced that the ideal social structure was indeed integration, yet this did not lead him to abandon the idea of black economics and nationalism. Malcolm also expressed sympathy for his former beliefs from a sociological standpoint rather than a religious one.

> I believe in recognizing every human being as a human being—neither white, black, brown, or red; and when you are dealing with humanity there's no question of integration or intermarriage...I don't think the burden to defend any position should ever be put upon the black man, because it is the white man collectively who has shown that he is hostile toward integration and toward intermarriage and toward these other strides toward oneness. So as a black man and especially as a black American, any stand that I formerly took, I don't think I would have to defend it because it's still a reaction that was produced by the society; and I think that it is the society that produced this that should be attacked, not the reaction that develops among the people who are the victims of that negative society.[41]

This was the direction that Wallace Muhammad moved the

41

black-Muslim movement. It would become a movement that would continue to embrace black consciousness, but it would be far in the background of the religious culture. No other leader in American history had accomplished the task of bringing about such a sudden movement of tens of thousands of its citizens into orthodox Islam. In fact, the majority of the natural born orthodox Muslims today are of the black-Muslim variety which descended from the work of Wallace Muhammad. Upon his death, Wallace Muhammad was viewed as a major historical and religious figure in American life by the news media. Of course, Wallace Muhammad's movement was not ultimately called the Nation of Islam, but rather the American Muslim Mission. The name "Nation of Islam" was changed soon after he assumed leadership. Farrakhan has also publicly expressed the reason why he rejects the reforms of Wallace, according to Vibert White's accounting:

> Farrakhan had preached that the 'Arab way of Islam is not the NOI way. The Messenger taught us, the Nation, that we don't have to pray or worship like you. You, Arab, prostrate yourself because you have an evil nature. The black man is good by nature, he is a God. Thus, you're trying to be what we are by nature— righteous.[42]

It was for these reasons that Farrakhan revived the Elijah Muhammad principles and hundreds who had left because of the changes brought on by his son, flocked back to the renewed Nation of Islam. This likely was due to the early appeal for racial solidarity and group consciousness. Those who were attracted to the old

---

[42] White, 62.

mindset began to return and reorganize under Farrakhan's leadership. However, after years of seeking to revive the legacy of Elijah Muhammad, Farrakhan began to move his sect in the direction of Wallace Muhammad while maintaining the old culture of the Nation of Islam. Farrakhan began to diminish the importance of Elijah Muhammad as a divine prophetic figure, and more as a historical founder of a divinely called movement. Fard Muhammad, the predecessor of Elijah Muhammad, was no longer considered by Farrakhan as the incarnation of God. However, in contrast with Wallace Muhammad, according to Vibert L. White, the evolution of Farrakhan may have been more a political than a spiritual transformation of mind.

> Another issue that clashed with the Nation's theology was Farrakhan's demotion of its two greatest leaders, Fard Muhammad and Elijah Muhammad, from being divinities of the Quran to being merely great Muslim leaders. Farrakhan's reversal was motivated by Qadhafi's and the Nations need for support among traditional Islamic leaders and groups. Orthodox Muslims, as they are called, had much greater education, wealth, and international influence than did Farrakhan's all black nation. Qadhafi and Farrakhan desperately needed these individuals and organizations to make an impact on Western society and politics. However, before the Nation could attract these traditionalists, Farrakhan had to make theological concessions.[43]

Farrakhan is often viewed as straddling a theological tightrope between orthodox Islam and the old Nation of Islam theology. This confusion has impeded if not hurt the progress of the Nation of Islam

---

[43] Ibid, 185.

in its most recent phase. If Elijah Muhammad is not divine and Fard Muhammad is not God incarnated, then the very existence of the Nation of Islam has no basis or foundation. This has been Farrakhan's challenge. The true believers in Elijah Muhammad are uncomfortable with his reversals, so he must placate them as much as possible.

The Muslim-American world created by Wallace Muhammad and the public at large are uncomfortable with Elijah's strange theology, therefore Farrakhan seems to attempt accommodating them also. One of these theological positions goes beyond the idea of the supposed divinity of Fard and Elijah, but it is one built upon the concept of black- scientists, UFOs, and the return of the dead. Most non-Muslim black intellectuals can embrace the Nation of Islam's concepts of pride of self and community, but the UFO belief is where many begin to part ways with the philosophy of Farrakhan. However, he seems to feel the need to return to such ideas in order to assure the true believers. His critics within his movement are uncomfortable with Farrakhan's drive to promote Arab nationalism, when the movement is founded on black-nationalism and Elijah Muhammad's beliefs. Farrakhan lectures upon topics that will appeal to followers of Elijah Muhammad in order to prove that he is also a believer. The following was observed by Vibert White.

> [Responding to criticism for turning to Arab nationalism and away from Elijah, he refers to the Nation of Islam belief that]... a spaceship occupied by twenty-four black scientists orbited the earth. Belief in this UFO, or mother plane is central to the theology of the Nation. Between 1981 and 1984 Farrakhan delivered scores of lectures on the mother

plane. Sensing the criticism of his activities with Qadhafi and other Arab leaders, Farrakhan temporarily went back to Elijah's teachings of the mother plane. Farrakhan's return to the issue of UFOs was illustrated in an alleged vision of Elijah Muhammad and the mother plane...Farrakhan claimed at a 1984 press conference in Washington, D.C., that during one of his frequent vacations at his Mexican villa, he was beamed aboard the mother plane. Stating that this was a vision, he maintained that he met with Elijah Muhammad...alive and in good health. More important, however, Elijah stated that President Reagan, Vice President Bush, and General Colin Powell and other members of the Joint Chiefs of staff had developed a plan to attack Libya and to exterminate Black Americans...Two years later in December the Reagan administration attacked Libya...In addition, Farrakhan argued that the crack explosion in Black America was part of the government's plan to murder black Americans. Years later the minister maintained that he actually was transported to the spacecraft.[44]

It cannot be absolutely stated that the larger international Muslim world despises the disciplines and programs of the Nation of Islam. In the past, Muslim politicians from foreign countries have sought to use the Nation to lobby for their causes in America. In addition, foreign Muslim leaders have also been avid students of the recruitment practices of the Nation of Islam. Dannin observes the following:

> The Sunni Muslims even borrowed many of the tested recruiting methods of the Nation of Islam and incorporated them into their prison dawa programs, but they refused any and all association with the heretical teachings of Elijah Muhammad.[45]

---

[44] Ibid, 108.
[45] Dannin, 16.

Nonetheless, Farrakhan's straddling the fence between orthodox Islam and the old teaching of the Nation is thought to be one of the reasons for the diminishing numbers in the Nation of Islam. Wallace Muhammad's descendants far outnumber the followers of Farrakhan's Nation due to the confusion created by the constantly changing positions. The teachings of Wallace Muhammad are clear and easy to follow unlike that of Farrakhan's. White, the former leader in the movement, states, "In essence, Warith Deen Muhammad's track record of hating the theology and promising to bury his father's teachings is better than Farrakhan's bumpy ride of embracing two diametrically opposed religious ideas."[46]

The Nation of Islam did not practice Ramadan in its early days, which is a major feature of faith in the Muslim world. Today in order to compete with the ideals of Wallace Muhammad and to work closely with Muslim leaders abroad, the Nation is beginning to embrace Ramadan. However, the black-Muslims had earlier practiced another spiritual discipline in the place of Ramadan, which was a reaction to the excesses of society. Vibert White explains this NOI ethic.

> Under the leadership of Elijah Muhammad, the Nation did not observe the Muslim month of Ramadan...The Black Muslims fasted the month to illustrate the hypocrisy of Christians. Elijah Muhammad argued that Black Muslims fast during December because Christians overindulge in eating and drinking. He claimed that during this month so-

---

[46] White, 62.

called Christians get drunk and kill in the name of Jesus.[47]

If it were not for the concepts brought to light by Wallace Muhammad, would the Nation of Islam still embrace a closer connection to the tenants of orthodox Islam?

Farrakhan has also evolved over time in many other ways as well. He does not refer to whites as devils as in the past, but rather attacks the system of white supremacy. One strange feature that has made black leaders uncomfortable about Farrakhan's message is his pivot away from addressing white supremacy to chasing Jewish conspiracy theories and their relationship to black suffering. Despite this development, Farrakhan is widely seen as a figure who has moderated as he has aged. Could this moderation be the result of changes in society, and the Nation of Islam's attempt to adjust to the change?

---

[47] Ibid, 111.

6 Social Protest Movement or Religion?

Is the Nation of Islam primarily a social protest movement or a religious one? This is an important question. Those outside of the black-Muslim movement are not necessarily drawn to its religious rhetoric but admire the courage of their social protest. It would be difficult to find admirers or followers who would be drawn to the religious aspect alone while dismissing the social protest. When listening to the public speeches of Elijah Muhammad, Malcolm X, or Louis Farrakhan, one may find more rhetoric in the arena of social reform, social justice and historical perspective that one would hear about spirituality.

The Nation of Islam forbade their adherents to get involved with U. S. politics, yet its founder had a very political dimension in his teachings. The speeches of Nation of Islam leaders no doubt had an impact on the politics of their hearers whether Muslim or Non-Muslim. Pan-Africanism and Pan-Islam are political concepts in their very nature. Richard Brent Turner observed the following:

> As a sharp political thinker, Fard recognized the connections between Pan- Africanism and Pan-Islam. Since the time of Edward W. Blyden, some Pan- Africanists had favored Islam. The political discourses of the movements were similar—both sought to make sense of the cultures of non-white peoples who had been subjected to colonialism and slavery and formulated international coalitions to oppose Western imperialism and to empower Africans and

Asians.[48]

Malcolm X and Elijah Muhammad are noted in history as having a limited involvement within the sphere of international Politics. With any religion, it is nearly impossible to deny the political impact of its value system. This is the case no matter how much a religious body claims to avoid politics. Wherever there are mutual causes among groups of religious people, politics always comes into the picture. C. Eric Lincoln identifies these connections in the following:

> Like Christianity and Judaism, Islam is more than a religion: it has served also as a political force, drawing together coalitions of states for various purposes at various times. Today it is dynamically important in shaping political alignments among Moslem nations from Morocco to Indonesia.[49]

When thinking individuals consider politics, one almost immediately thinks about governmental aspects; there is also the politics of religion to consider. In the history of the Nation of Islam there was competition between them and the extremely tiny followers of mainstream Islam. The majority of those who professed Islam in America were among the followers of Elijah Muhammad. During the rise of the Nation of Islam there was an effort by the minority mainstream Muslim believers to bar them from Mecca. Their argument was that the black-Muslims were not authentic followers of the Koran. The foreign leaders understood the good

---

[48] Turner, 172.
[49] Lincoln, 224.

politics of allowing the so-called unorthodox black- Muslim acceptance into Mecca. Lincoln illustrates this reality in the following scenario:

[Cairo, Mecca, UAR] That these visits of Muslim leaders to the Islamic countries have political implications remains open to speculation. However, it is reasonable to conclude that the controversial Muslim leader could hardly have been admitted to Mecca in the face of the opposition of American Moslems unless he had powerful friends abroad to sponsor and receive him. Because of his heterodoxy, that sponsorship is unlikely to have been primarily religious. It seems possible that some Moslem leaders, at least, found the political possibilities sufficiently impressive to overbalance the religious risk.[50]

Black Islam was a more powerful voice in American than orthodox Islam, therefore was more attractive to foreign leaders. The international Muslim world understood that the Nation of Islam had a greater ability to impact politics in America in their favor than any other professors of Islamic faith in America. They understood that even though the black- Muslims were supposedly apolitical, their influence on politics could not be underestimated. The black-Muslims needed the international community for their own validation, and the international Muslim world needed the NOI to represent their own causes. The black Muslims spoke up against the American political system, European colonialism, and unjust wars. This was the voice that they needed in America even if its impact was minimal. Lincoln goes into further detail in the following

---

[50] Ibid, 227.

statement:

> To build an effective bloc in the United States, therefore, the Moslem states would have to convert large numbers of American citizens to Islam—and this the Black Muslims are doing with evident success. The orthodox Moslem bodies in America are dwarfed by Black Islam, and their cries of protest are likely to fall on apathetic ears in the important Islamic capitals of the East...They have their Mecca, and they have Medina, but Elijah has Chicago. And New York. And Los Angeles.[51]

One of the more interesting features of social change is how various religions adapt to the world in which they live. In some cases, religions are willing to relax some of their strongly held values in order to meet the challenges of the day. In the early days of the Nation of Islam, voting for politicians was considered an evil that should be avoided. It was not until Malcolm X left the Nation of Islam to become more active in the civil rights movement that he began to advocate for blacks having the right to vote. The Nation of Islam considers themselves a nation within a nation and should not become involved with attempting to place leaders in office through voting. Farrakhan, who by the late 80s had reestablished the Nation of Islam in America, began to advocate for black-Muslims voting.

An interesting development occurred during the 1988 Democratic primary. Jesse Jackson entered the primary as a candidate for the Democratic nomination for president of the United States. Michael Dukakis was the favored candidate in the race and Jesse Jackson was polling as a strong second option candidate. This

---

[51] Lincoln, 224 and 227.

was indeed a historic election for a black American to advance so far in a presidential election season. Jesse Jackson was known as for his advocacy of civil rights during the late stages of Dr. Martin Luther King's programs for the poor. Farrakhan understood the historical significance of such an event and adjusted the NOI's former position against voting in American elections. This was an obvious attempt to become a part of the history and to lend support to Jackson. Farrakhan endorsed the Jackson candidacy which was an unprecedented move for black-Muslims. The Nation of Islam mobilized its followers on Jackson's behalf. The Fruit of Islam, a para-military security apparatus of the Nation of Islam, provided security for Jackson during his campaign travels. Farrakhan even threatened that if anyone sought to harm Jesse Jackson in pursuit of the presidency that blacks and NOI members would retaliate against those enemies. Lincoln recalls those times in the following words:

> Perhaps Farrakhan's most far-reaching development was leading the Nation to full participation in the political life of America...In 1990 three members of the Nation ran for political office in Washington, D. C., a move that did not go unnoticed in the inner circles of national and political leadership.[52]

One of the more controversial political actions of Farrakhan, following the historic Million Man March, was his world tour through the Middle East and Africa. To the dismay of white politicians as well as black civil rights leaders, America's most hated enemies were visited and embraced by Farrakhan. While on

---

[52] Ibid, 271.

his whirlwind tour Farrakhan publicly denounced the foreign policies of America. Countries such as Cuba, Sudan, Iraq, Iran and Libya were among the countries where he made his presence felt. Farrakhan may have felt that his was leveraging his credibility as an American leader to gain aid and support for black America, but others felt that he was allowing himself to be used as a tool of America's enemies. White recounts the events of the international tour and the subsequent reaction in the United States in the following:

> Farrakhan's most steaming diatribe came in Libya, when he verbally accepted a $1 billion pledge from Qadhafi to mobilize blacks, Arabs, Muslims, and Native Americans to influence America's foreign policy and to exert pressure on the ultimate outcome of the presidential elections. In referring to the Libyan president as his friend and Muslim brother, Farrakhan endorsed Quadafi's views that Farrakhan and the Nation could become Qadhafi's agent within the fortress called the United States.

> Despite this reaction by the political establishment in the United States, Farrakhan continued to be admired by those who viewed him as an honest advocate. This crisis did not win him any favors within the mainstream of American society, but rendered further street cred to those who viewed the American government with mistrust.

7 The Attraction of Non-Muslims to The Nation

What many in the white political establishment as well as mainstream American thinkers are puzzled about is the attraction of black non-Muslims to the causes of Louis Farrakhan. In 1992, an audience of 60,000 attended a Louis Farrakhan event. What many do not realize is that Farrakhan was mentored and taught by Malcolm X--a cultural icon. Farrakhan sounds and speaks very similarly to Malcolm and is the closest reminder of the late minister. There are also those who blame him for his rhetoric against Malcolm shortly before his death. He publicly declared Malcolm as one who is worthy of death shortly before his assassination in 1965. Farrakhan later embraced the legacy of Malcolm.

Farrakhan's reputation as an unfiltered and courageous spokesperson for black America has survived myriad controversies throughout his tenure as NOI leader. He continues to be a sought after speaker wherever he travels in the United States among the black populace. Lincoln dispels the notion that Farrakhan's appeal is limited to former convicts.

> Who goes to hear Farrakhan? The notion that his audiences are confined to down-and-outers from the inner city is misleading. But many of those who go to hear Farrakhan are ordinary middle-class African Americans who

do not think of themselves as candidates for recruitment but who have a vague sense of obligation to hear what he has to say, nonetheless. Few commit themselves, but even fewer are willing to denounce Farrakhan as a charlatan or dismiss him as a fool...It is perhaps Farrakhan's inexplicable attractiveness to the responsible element of the black community that constitutes the major source of threat and irritation that the Muslim leader seems to pose.[53]

There are a number of features which attract non-Muslims to the work of the Nation of Islam: its ability to mobilize for causes of concern in the black community to influence the American public, its education in the area of black heritage, history, cultural sensitivity and discipline of Muslim Schools,[54] its newspaper publication which addresses issues of black concern in America and in the world and is aggressively disseminated. Lincoln calls the Final Call newspaper "the largest circulation of any black periodical in the country."[55]

The Muslims' power to influence the general American community is significant, not only because of their increasing financial resources, but also because they can be mobilized to act in unswerving unison on any matter designated by leadership[56]

Another area which may explain the appeal of Farrakhan is the fact that there are very few black leaders that the inner-city residents feel that they can trust. Farrakhan has filled this void. This may explain how it was ever conceivable that someone as controversial

---

[53] Lincoln, 270.
[54] Ibid, 31.
[55] Ibid, 272.
[56] Ibid, 18.

as Louis Farrakhan could lead the largest march of black men ever witnessed in America. The Million Man March was significant in its size and its accomplishment. The last such march occurred in 1963 where Martin Luther King Jr. delivered his "I Have a Dream Speech."

The Million Man March may not be remembered for its speeches, but for its ability to mobilize so many for a spiritual cause in such a short amount of time. The NAACP, Jesse Jackson, black intellectuals, Hollywood actors, and other Christian ministers helped Farrakhan lead the event. Lincoln describes the focus and spirit of the march in the following words:

> ...word of the march captured the imagination of the black community at the midnight hour.... African American males boarded planes, buses, automobiles, trains, and some even walked hundreds of miles to attend the greatest black march demonstration in history. Although Farrakhan thought these men came because of his leadership and appeal for religious atonement, they came rather because of the growth of black solidarity and the absence of black leaders. Unfortunately, African Americans lacked race advocates such as A. Phillip Randolph, Thurgood Marshall, Ralph Abernathy, and Martin Luther King Jr. to aggressively challenge American racism in the 1990s.[57]

What will be Farrakhan's legacy? Will he be considered a leader of black America or a leader of a strange sect of Elijah Muhammad followers? What will be his greatest accomplishment on the public stage? He is a man who is viewed as a cancer in society by some and a healer by others. He has been involved in organizing gang truces

---

[57] White, 167, 168.

in the inner cities and has launched many social help programs. Time will most certainly tell. For now, the Million Man March will perhaps be viewed for generations to come as the legacy that will follow. Vibert White has the following commentary on the historical magnitude of the event:

> The Million Man March opened up both a can of worms and a world of opportunities for Farrakhan. It defined his moment in American history. Scholars of history, political science, and religion cannot ignore the great feat that Louis Farrakhan accomplished in spearheading over one million black men to the District of Columbia. After the one-day event the Muslim leader became the ultimate black leader of the United States.[58]

Despite the fact that the black-Muslims reject Christianity, many would use the bible in their early days in their recruitment efforts. Black Muslim leaders are also known to quote the words of Jesus as they appeal to the black public. Is this paradox a matter of Christianity influencing black-Muslims or black-Muslims influencing the black church? Today, it is quite normal to hear black-Muslims speak favorably of the black church and to speak more reverently concerning Christ. This was not necessarily true in their early days. Dannin explains the attraction in the following statement:

> Neither the Moors nor the Nation of Islam practice Islam in any conventional sense…Sociologists have suggested that both groups incorporated many Christian elements into their beliefs to attract greater numbers of blacks to their essentially secular programs of political and economic

---

[58] White, 185.

nationalism. Others have viewed the politics of the Nation of Islam, especially the rhetoric of Malcolm X, as the 'antithesis of the assimilationist civil rights doctrine' of the 1960s and a rejection of the 'turn the other cheek' dictum of the black church.[59]

Others suggest that the black-Muslims' Christian lingo was a result of the environment in which they existed. This may not be the case in Muslim countries, but the Nation of Islam is an American idea in a Christian setting. The Christian concepts which the black-Muslims express are both for recruitment purposes as well as a natural outflow of their Christian background. Many of the adherents have their background in the churches of protestant America. African American Muslims appropriated many older, sometimes explicitly Christian themes of black uplift and recast them in an Islamic mold.[60] Lincoln adds to the explanation for the paradox.

> Except for the Moorish-Americans and a few hundred ex-cultists of varying past proclivities, most of the Muslims seem to be drawn from Protestant families or traditions…Many Muslims have come from revivalist sects, but most have held active membership in the established denominations, and some of the Muslim ministers are former Christian preachers.[61]

Such a movement could only be birthed in a Slavery-believing

---

[59] Dannin, 170.
[60] Curtis, 97.
[61] Lincoln, 25.

Christian, Anglo dominated, and anti-black society. Although the movement thrives as a protest movement against slave-holding Christianity and a passive black middle class Christianity, the influence of the religious society in America may be seen in the language and traditions in the black Muslim movement.

8 Good Cop – Bad Cop

In order for the majority population to understand the shared psychology of the black-American church, one must understand the mindset of group consciousness. Under certain extreme moments in society, group consciousness will cause a minority to dismiss their denominational and religious differences to confront particular issues which are hurting that minority group as a whole. An example of this can be found in the 1954 Montgomery bus boycott; it should be noted that Rosa Parks was a Methodist and Dr. King was a Baptist. During the 1963 March on Washington many different Christian denominations were present, including Roman Catholics. In King's "I Have a Dream Speech," he referenced the coming together of "Jews and Gentiles, Protestants and Catholics." This will explain the dynamic of why Farrakhan has received invitations to speak in black churches in the inner city and why the Nation of Islam has joined causes led by Christian preachers in the inner cities. In those cases, even group consciousness trumped religion.

What is the definition of "group consciousness?" Lincoln describes the meaning of this term. He points out that this "group consciousness" can be the consequence of either a demographic or economic majority. He shows how that a minority population with supreme economic power can have the same effects on a minority as does a demographic majority. He points out the extreme consequences of the abuses which come about when a group has both economic as well as demographic power.

> An interesting phenomenon found in every society in which discrete groups live side by side is known as consciousness of kind, that state of mind in which individuals are vividly aware of themselves as members of a group different from other groups...Consciousness of kind usually operates as a defense mechanism for a minority group that is seeking to preserve its identity or its most cherished values...The group consciousness of a minority is, of course, increased by acts of discrimination directed against it by an effective majority. An effective majority need not be a numerical majority: 250,000 Europeans constitute an effective majority in the African state of Rhodesia, which they share with the five million Africans, and 3.5 million Europeans are an effective majority in South Africa, a country of fifteen million Blacks. An effective majority, whatever its size, holds the main concentration of power...When it enjoys actual power backed by a massive numerical superiority—as does the white majority in the United States— the group consciousness of the minority can be very sharp indeed.[62]

This same "consciousness-of-kind" may be the reason why various social, religious, and political groups which embrace different tactics feel as sense of unity among each other and come together on certain issues. The black-Muslims speak favorably about the black Hebrew Israelites, The black Hebrew Israelites speak favorably about the black Muslims and the civil rights establishment. The Civil Rights establishment shows respect for the black Muslims and the black Hebrew Israelites.

---

[62] Lincoln, 33,34.

The same mindset by which black ministers feel "the call" to preach may be the same motivation for blacks to join the Muslim movement. It has been historically difficult for black leaders to exercise their leadership strengths through the mainstream political system. Many who had the gift to become lawyers, politicians and educators were often held back due to systemic barriers. The black clergy was therefore historically the hallmark of black professionalism. Through the black church those who desired to have a voice in society and effect change would find their forum and voice to do so. It also created a comfort zone for black leaders to be regarded with respect and to find encouragement for their efforts. They were admired among congregants who were proud of their accomplishments.

Some may suggest it was through the black church that black American leadership was allowed to flourish. The black-Muslim movement is based on the same concept; if it were not for the existence of economic exploitation and second-class citizenship, black-Muslim leaders would not have been necessary. Black Christian clergy and black-Muslim ministers have the same roots and are the consequence of the same societal dynamics. Many black congressmen are also and were once church ministers, and Lincoln draws the connection between public service and black religion.

> The black church was the one significant mitigating organization that stood between black people and the utter hopelessness of slavery, and it has remained the prime source of strength and leadership for black dissent ever since. To some extent the church was and is escapist. E. Franklin Frazier observes that it "has two roots: one in the

efforts of the free Negroes in the North to escape from their inferior position in white churches and assert their independence, and the other in what has been aptly called the 'invisible' institution on the plantations during slavery." Benjamin Mays concludes that 'if the Negro had had greater freedom in the social, economic, and political spheres, fewer Negroes would have been 'called' to preach, and there would have been fewer Negro churches.[63]

While the idea of black-Muslim religion may seem odd to some and ridiculous to others in American society, the black church's emphasis on "consciousness of kind" is quite similar to that of the Muslims. The black church is not viewed with the same suspicion because the nature of its solidarity is based on American Christian principles. This similarity demonstrates that Muslims are not alone in their reactions to the perceived exploitation and disenfranchisement by society. However, the black American churches do not have the same shock value on the larger society. The sociological paradox stems from the fact that both white society and the majority of black Americans profess Christianity, yet the minority group is reacting to what they view as un-Christ-like values of the majority. Another interesting development is that the black-Muslims share many of the social values of evangelical Christianity such as self-reliance, small-government, entrepreneurship, anti-Hollywood, traditional families, and conservative lifestyle practices. Nonetheless, the Muslim emphasis on black unity causes many in the Evangelical world to overlook their shared values and may have

---

[63] Ibid, 235.

never noticed they exist. Lincoln shows the connection between the religious rhetoric of the black Muslim movement and black Christian theology with its focus upon black dignity and liberation.

> The theological basis of the Muslim social doctrine reflect in part the extraordinary degree of their alienation from the American mainstream. The contemporary preoccupation of black Christians with 'black theology' and 'black religion' suggests a deepening sense of estrangement throughout the whole black community and the increasing acceptability of the notion of separate identity and hence a separate destiny, The Black Muslims and the black Christians alike reject the white Christian's age-old presumption of superiority, and 'black theology,' Christian or Muslim, is in part a response to the African American's interpretation of the way white American Christians perceive reality and order their system of values.[64]

Although in today's world, the Civil Rights movement is viewed historically with admiration and respect, this was not always the case during the 60s. Many Americans accepted and agreed with the goals of the movement but disagreed with their tactics of direct action. Others saw them as being impatient for change in America. History informs its students that J. Edgar Hoover and the FBI viewed Dr. Martin Luther King as a threat to the social fabric of America and watched him closely. In addition, there were those in America who opposed both the goals and the tactics of the movement. How were Civil Rights leaders successful in their aims? How was it possible that they were able to gain the ear of

---

[64] Ibid, 250-251

government officials? In many ways it can be stated that the more militant figures in black America aided their civil rights counterparts in ways that cannot be measured. How did the black-Muslim movement help the civil rights movement? An example of this can be best illustrated in the words of Malcolm X in one of his conversations with Alex Haley.

> I was waiting for another plane to Kansas City to witness the swearing-in of my youngest brother George who had recently been elected a Kansas State Senator, 'Tell your brother for me to remember us in the alley,' Malcolm X said, 'Tell him that he and all of the other moderate Negroes who are getting somewhere need to always remember that it was us extremists who made it possible.'[65]

Malcolm X, after his break with the Nation of Islam, had a great desire to join the efforts of civil rights leaders in the South. He particularly desired to meet with Dr. King. On one occasion he angled to shake hands and to appear in a photo with King, which is the only meeting and photo of the two together. Could it be that Malcolm was seeking to send a message to the political establishment? Is it possible that while King may have been shy about such an encounter, that he may have in fact appreciated it? During the weeks prior to Malcolm's assassination, he joined a campaign in Alabama with other civil rights leaders. It was his hope that he would meet King on this trip, but King was in jail during this time. Many of the black leaders were nervous about the presence of

---

[65] Haley, 486.

Malcolm, yet he was treated with respect. They did not want the public to perceive their efforts with Malcolm X's rhetoric on the right to bear arms and self-defense for blacks. They were fearful that his presence may be a setback for their cause, and that potential violence could occur. Some may suggest that the leaders needed Malcolm as much as he needed them. Although they may have been nervous, Malcolm viewed himself as being helpful. Jet Magazine, as referenced by Lincoln, reports on what would next take place during this visit and its possible sociological impact.

Jet magazine reported Malcolm X's trip to Selma, Alabama, on the invitation of two members of the Student Nonviolent Coordinating Committee. Dr. Martin Luther King was in a Selma jail when Malcolm X's arrival sent officials of Dr. King's Southern Christian Leadership Conference 'into a tailspin.' At the church where he would speak, Malcolm X was seated on the platform next to Mrs. Martin Luther King, to whom he leaned and whispered that he was 'trying to help,' she told Jet, 'He said he wanted to present an alternative; that it might be easier for whites to accept Martin's proposals after hearing him (Malcolm X). I didn't understand him at first,' said Mrs. King. 'He seemed rather anxious to let Martin know he was not causing trouble or making it difficult, but that he was trying to make it easier...Later, in the hallway, he reiterated this. He seemed sincere...'" Addressing the mass meeting, Malcolm X reportedly shouted: 'I don't advocate violence, but if a man steps on my toes, I'll step on his.'... 'Whites better be glad Martin Luther King is rallying the people because other forces are waiting to take over if he fails.'[66]

Reverend Fred Shuttlesworth recalled the Malcolm X visit at the

---

[66] Ibid, 490-491

Brown's Chapel AME church. Shuttlesworth, although little known today, was a significant and almost indispensable figure during the movement. Shuttlesworth was such a vocal advocate for black rights that he kindled the ire of the Ku Klux Klan in Alabama. On one occasion his home was bombed and he managed to make it out alive. This brought him great respect as a warrior for the movement. During the Malcolm X visit, the ideas of self-defense and non-violence clashed. Despite this, the public did not understand the dynamics of the good cop, bad cop psychology between the two philosophies playing out in the American consciousness.

The Martin Luther King philosophy advanced the idea of non-retaliation against violent enemies, and that the public would then be able to identify the immorality of civil rights opponents, witness their suffering of blacks, and sympathize with their efforts and goals. The philosophy suggested that any efforts at self-defense would confuse the public about who were the true enemies of society. Shuttlesworth described King's philosophy as "the redemptive power of unearned suffering." The philosophy assumed that society would always side with the underdog. Both Malcolm and Shuttlesworth shared the same goals but disagreed upon tactical maneuvers. The fact that Malcolm was welcomed onto the stage among Christian ministers was also a major development. Malcolm X came in support of King, and wanted the public to fear his alternative methods for change and consequently embrace King's efforts. Andrew Manis, who authored an award winning biography about Rev. Fred Shuttlesworth, describes the encounter in the following words:

> In early February (1965) Shuttlesworth visited a rally in Selma, speaking to a group of three hundred, which was composed primarily of high school students. Preceding him at the podium was Malcolm X, who in this instance was participating in one of his few active involvements in the mainstream civil rights movement. Malcolm arrived with an entourage of reporters, warning that if Dallas County officials did not heed King's requests, he would come in with his army. Shuttlesworth privately dismissed Malcolm's claim and knew Malcolm was playing on white fears of the Black Muslims. When he introduced the crowd at Brown's Chapel AME church, he advised the press to note in particular the contrast between Malcolm's methods and those of the SCLC. [Shuttlesworth] told the audience that his many trials in the movement had convinced him all the more of King's idea of the redemptive power of unearned suffering.[67]

Shuttlesworth, Mr. and Mrs. King, the SCLC and other traditional Civil Rights organizations understood the value of having militant voices such as Malcolm's in the public square. Malcolm's discourse took the lid off of black anger which had long been hidden, helped all parties navigate the psychology of white anger and simultaneously made those involved in militant direct action appear reasonable and statesmen-like.

---

[67] Andrew Manis, *A Fire You Can't Put Out--The Civil Rights Life of Birmingham's Reverend Fred Shuttleswoth* (Tuscaloosa, Alabama: University of Alabama Press, 1999), 418.

9 The Legacy of The Nation of Islam in America

The Nation of Islam has had peaks and valleys in its publicly visible presence on the national scene in its history in America. Its initial peak came with the 50s Mike Wallace documentary, the presence of Malcolm X in Harlem in the 1960s, the Jesse Jackson and Mike Dukakis Democratic primary in 1988, and the Million Man March. The break with Malcolm X and Elijah Muhammad was perhaps its most painful time. The assassination of Malcolm X gave the Nation of Islam a metaphorical "black eye" from which they have never healed. It is very significant that Betty Shabazz, the widow of Malcolm, participated in the Million Man March. In between those peak moments, the Nation of Islam has largely fallen from the consciousness of America.

Louis Farrakhan is now elderly and no longer the firebrand that he once was and does not gain the national attention that he once enjoyed. He became a topic of conversation during the 2008 election season as he publicly endorsed Barack Obama at the Nation's annual Savior's Day Convention. During the debates, Senator Obama was asked whether he embraced the endorsement of Farrakhan. Obama was criticized because he did not outright condemn Farrakhan when asked. Could it be that Obama was hesitant because he understood the goodwill that the Nation of Islam leader enjoyed within the black community which he needed for his election? It is also interesting to watch how the evolution of the Nation of Islam has over time gained them favor in the wider world of Islam. Thus, there are still political and religious impacts which result from the influence of the Nation of Islam. Lincoln adds the following concerning the evolution of the Nation of Islam, and its significance in America's future.

> The reconstruction of the Nation of Islam is complete and continuing. The Black Muslims are here to stay. They have earned their place within the widening spectrum of Islamic persuasions in America. But, more important in the long run, they are also an American persuasion in Islam.[68]

Another successor of Elijah Muhammad, his son Wallace Muhammad, has achieved more from a religious standpoint in America than has Louis Farrakhan. Another difference between Farrakhan and Wallace Muhammad is that Elijah Muhammad's son was never the firebrand that was Louis Farrakhan. Farrakhan gained much television coverage due to his controversial words and actions, while Wallace Muhammad was reserved and enjoyed most of his work behind the scenes. He may be considered the Muslim Billy Graham in America. It is interesting that despite the fact that Wallace Muhammad's movement was much larger, he did not get the same attention and notoriety of the smaller group which was the Nation of Islam. Vibert White reminds readers of the legacy of Muhammad in American history and his current impact on today's NOI.

---

[68] Lincoln, 271.

Warith Deen Muhammad has silently built the largest
Black Muslim community in the United States. His
American Mission Movement has achieved domestic and
international respect and admiration from political and
religious leaders and organizations. Although his views
differ from those of the earlier Farrakhan, they are similar to
the current more moderate Farrakhan.[69]

While the Nation of Islam appears to have moderated over the
years, there are still those critics who believe that Farrakhan is a
menace to society and that the Nation of Islam does not have a bright
future ahead. Farrakhan's moderation has led to a splintering and
rise of rival groups among the followers of Elijah Muhammad's
philosophy, yet former members continue to criticize Farrakhan for
being extreme. While C. Eric Lincoln believes the Nation of Islam
is here to stay, there are those who are doubtful about its future
prospects.

The future for Farrakhan's Nation is grim. His views are
controversial, the organization is structurally and financially
weak, its theology is unclear—changing from day to day and
audience to audience—and its politics are shaped by
Farrakhan's personal friend Qadhafi. If things do not change
for the better, Farrakhan's organization will not survive the
twenty-first century...As it stands now, Farrakhan's group
will undergo the same sad death as Marcus Garvey's
Universal Negro Improvement Association, Noble Drew
Ali's Moorish Science Temple Movement, and Father
Divine's Peace Mission Organization.[70]

---

[69] White, 205.
[70] Ibid, 207.

It may be easy to dismiss the Garvey Association and the Moorish Temple as faded memories of bygone eras, but the historical impacts of those movements are still felt. It is not always easy to predict the future of any particular sect or social movement in society, because it is difficult to predict events that give power to certain movements. It may appear that a movement has faded from the scene, yet a singular earth-shattering event in the world may bring them back into prominence. For example, Farrakhan was close to Libyan leader Qadafi, so when America participated in the military campaign against Qadafi, Farrakhan once again found his public voice. Qadafi was eventually killed during that campaign. Farrakhan gave voice to what he believed were sinister political motivations for the Libyan invasion. There may be other similar events that will arise.

While there may be those who cannot understand why a black-Muslim movement ever came into being, the reasons often lie beneath the surface. Those who adhere to the philosophy may not consciously understand the factors by which they are drawn. Is it the religion of black-Muslims that black Americans find attractive or is the social protest feature that is the main drawing card? To understand these dynamics, one must refer to Lincoln's observation concerning "consciousness-of-kind."

> The fundamental attraction of the Black Muslim movement is its passion for group solidarity, its exaggerated sense of consciousness-of-kind…the ultimate appeal of the movement, therefore, is the chance to become identified with a power strong enough to overcome the domination of whites—and perhaps even to subordinate them in turn…in

this context, although the Black Muslims call their movement a religion, religious values have a secondary importance. They are not part of the movement's basic appeal, except to the extent that they foster and strengthen the sense of group solidarity.[71]

This idea of group solidarity may also be compared to the Eastern European "Solidarity Movement" of the late 1980s, which brought down the iron curtain and the eventual fall of the Soviet empire. This was also a religiously led movement driven by the politics of the Roman Catholic Church under Pope John Paul II. While the "Solidarity" movement brought about dramatic visible change in Eastern Europe, it may be that the impact of the Nation of Islam was a more of a subtle, political, inspirational, and educational dynamic in America.

---

[71] Lincoln, 26.

10 Black Theology Black Pride and Black Religion

When analyzing the presence of black nationalism, and the widespread interest in black consciousness and Pan-Africanism, the Nation of Islam remains influential. According to Damon Richardson, an urban Christian apologist and former member of the Nation of Islam, black cultural events and black artists continue to have the support of Farrakhan and members of the Nation of Islam. This relationship between black culture and the NOI buoys the popularity of its leader within the larger community, many of which are members of the black church. Richardson asserts that this symbiosis creates a social bond due to mutual love for the black community and its redemption. The ties between black Christian culture and the NOI are not due to religious dogma but black familyhood.

As a former member of the NOI, who grew up in the movement, Richardson acknowledges that the attraction to Farrakhan by the broader black community is due to what is viewed as fearless leadership. As Richardson sees it, unlike mainstream black leaders and politicians, Farrakhan appears to be totally liberated from attempts to appease the white establishment. While many black Americans, according to Richardson, are suspicious of black politicians, they feel that Farrakhan will say what other leaders cannot. Vilification of Farrakhan by the American media only strengthens his "street cred" within the African American community, according to Richardson.

Richardson suggests that Farrakhan's credibility remains solid. This is because most are convinced that his love for the black community is unquestioned and that he has the answers to many of the inter and intra racial problems which exist. A champion of the black underclass, as Richardson writes, is how Farrakhan is viewed. Consequently, it is observed that he has become the litmus test for the acceptance of black political aspirants in the white political realm. Black politicians are consistently quizzed on their views on Farrakhan in order gain the stamp of approval for the white public. Moreover, Richardson reveals that Farrakhan has toned down much of his early rhetoric. Richardson also highlights the reason why Farrakhan has found so much appreciation among black Christians:

Interfaith dialogue, politicized references, black cultural metaphors, event- oriented emphases, use of the Bible and Quran during teaching and public speeches and use traditional black rhetorical styles, often help Farrakhan feel right at home in many black churches where he preaches, and pushes NOI doctrines cloaked in Christian theological terminology and black church colloquialisms.[72]

While an early critic of the black church, Farrakhan has in most recent times sought greater connections than in the past. His

---

[72] Richardson, Damon, *Urban Apologetics-Restoring Black Dignity with the Gospel*, (E. Mason, Ed.) *(*Grand Rapids MI: Zondervan, 2021), 94-96.

appearance at black churches in the inner cities are extraordinarily more frequent than most leaders in the early days of the Muslim movement. Yet today, it is unclear if the NOI in its current form would qualify as a bad cop, as the legacy of black consciousness has been embraced by a large section of the community.

Martin Luther King Jr did not come across to White America as a good cop because he made them feel better about themselves, but because at least he spoke of love when the possibility of violent protest was real. King was not beloved for his work in the freedom struggle, because his direct-action efforts were so disruptive and threatened the status quo. He was despised by those who were afraid of the change that he would bring. The record shows that he was despised by both the Ku Klux Klan types as well as white moderates, but many were aware that there was an alternative which angrily critiqued White America and did not advocate for non-violent resistance. Influential media personality and professor of Sociology at Georgetown and Vanderbilt University, Michael Eric Dyson, reminds his readers that he also writes from the perspective of a Baptist clergyman. Dyson refers to White America's faux love affair with the legacy of Dr. King, stating in his book what a great number of white liberals and conservatives misunderstand. In his work, "Tears We Cannot Stop" he addressed America:

Beloved you say you love King, or at least admire him, but you don't really know him, not the King who was too black and too radical for America...King told the truth about you in black America, to black America, in ways he couldn't tell you. He said the toughest things about you in sacred black spaces. He did it because he felt safe with us...He understood what white folk could hear; he knew what you dared not listen to. He knew what you could bear to know. He understood the white psyche and when and how to pressure you to do the right thing. Early in his career King believed in the essential goodness of white America...In the last three years of his life, he concluded sadly, that most whites are unconscious racists.[73]

In other words, King was viewed as good cop because he avoided publicly speaking to and about White America in the same way a great many black people spoke in private. So, from the good cop, bad cop perspective, they hated King for his activism (He was not viewed as a "good guy,") but they hated Malcolm more. If they had to choose, they would choose King, being oblivious to the fact that they both shared the same views about the predominant society. Malcolm X was the most vocal and unfiltered of the two when naming and critiquing the problems of America. The same is true when it came to the demands of the black church and that of the black Muslims, while one appeared to be less threatening than the other, both were in fact a threat to the power structure.

Looking from the perspective of those outside of the black community, one might wrongly assume that the black church would have nothing to do with one claiming to be a Muslim. That Muslims are anti-Jesus is the understanding and perception of many American Christians. However, Muslims are considerably pro-

---

[73] Dyson, Michael Eric. *Tears We Cannot Stop*. (New York, New York: St. Martin's Press, 2017), 46-47.

Jesus; the difference is that they limit His ministry to that of a prophet. In fact, Orthodox Muslims reverence the name and personhood of Jesus, who won't mention His name without stating the words, "Peace be upon him." On this point, black Muslims and the Black church can agree; Jesus had a prophetic ministry. Black clergy related to the prophetic side of Jesus ministry which Malcolm emphasized. It must be remembered that in the black church tradition Jesus is not only God Incarnate, Savior and King, but he also has a prophetic ministry by which he prosecutes the powerful and identifies with and stands up for the marginalized, the disinherited and the poor. This was Malcolm's emphasis while speaking on behalf of the leader of the black Muslim movement within an interfaith gathering of black Muslims and black Christians in Los Angeles. They protested together a case of police brutality against Ronald Stokes.

In Los Angeles, Malcolm represented a more militant critique of white supremacy within the Police Department in Los Angeles. This locking of arms between the black Muslim movement and black Christians stoked fears of an alternatively militant response to the brutality than the traditional church based black civil rights movement. You will notice that there was little that any of the black clergy would disagree with in his depiction of a radical Jesus who stood in solidarity with the oppressed. Universal applause within the black community, is what any Jesus loving child of God, would render to anyone, Muslim or otherwise for such declarations. These were concepts that all who subscribed to black religion would rally behind: Malcolm X stated the following Christological views:

They charged Jesus with sedition! Didn't they do that? They said he was against Caesar. They said he was discriminating because he told his disciples 'Go not the way of the Gentiles. but go rather go to the lost sheep." He discriminated. Don't go near the Gentiles; go to the lost sheep. Go to the oppressed; Go to the exploited; go to the downtrodden. Go to the people who don't know who they are, and who are lost from the knowledge of themselves, and are strangers in a land that is not theirs. Go to these people. Go to the slaves. Go to the second-class citizens. Go to the ones who are suffering the brunt of Caesar's brutality. And if Jesus were here in America today, he wouldn't be going to the white man. The white man is the oppressor. He would be going to be oppressed. He would be going to the humble. He would be going to the lowly. He would be going to the rejected and the despised. He would be going to the so-called American Negro.[74]

This profound statement by Malcolm resonated with black clergy of all persuasions, because it represented the essence of black religion. Black religion has always been undergirded by a spiritual ethic which distinguishes between right and wrong in a racist society and utilizes its moral instincts and faith to resist white supremacy.

During the antebellum period in America and the reconstruction and Jim Crow era, the slave holder religion, which was embraced by white clergy, white ecclesiastical organizations, and mission groups, preached, taught and evangelized in ways to get black people to forget about challenging the systems that shackled and dehumanize them and to simply wait for their reward in heaven. The black

---

[74] Malcolm X, Speech Protesting Police Brutality against Ronald Stokes, Los Angeles CA, May 20, 1962

Muslim movement arose to push back against this emphasis to the degree that eschatologically they rejected the idea of an afterlife. They believed that black people were owed a section of land carved out of the North American continent where they could be free and independent of white rule and oppression. Expecting black people to focus on what had been owed them in "the here and now," and not in a future eschatological framework was a means of resistance.

In many cases, in the view of black Muslims and the more radical black clergy, it was insulting that such a great portion of both black preachers and white churches had given in to the notion of forgetting about present oppression and look forward to the day when there will be no more sorrow. As a result of this challenge, many black churches preachers and theologians began to adjust their emphasis in focusing on joy amid sorrow and addressing the present-day realities that were outside of God's divine order. This would be the answer to the prayer that was presented by Jesus in the gospel account where he taught us to pray "thy kingdom come thy will be done in earth as it is in heaven." In a few minor cases, quite like the black Muslims, some black theologians began to question the idea of the afterlife altogether to focus strictly on the need to build a righteous Kingdom on earth in the here and now.

One of the fathers of modern black theology, James Deotis Roberts, stated that the black Muslim movement was not actually orthodox Muslim due to its lack of alignment with the beliefs of the larger Muslim world, but rather was more closely aligned with black slave religion. He stated that it would qualify more so as a Christian heresy, which my well may be the reason the black Muslims we're able to hit a nerve and strike a chord by challenging black churches and black clergy. The black Muslim movement was a wake-up call within the black faith tradition. A pioneering voice and trailblazer of Black theological discourse in the late 1960's, J. Deotis Roberts, who authored several books, and taught in top level academic circles, made the following connection between black theology and the black Muslim movement. He refers to the critique of the black Muslims against the church's focus on the new heaven and new earth to act as tool to get black people to neglect the work of the here and now. The way Roberts sees it, the same mindset that gave rise to black theology within the church, also gave rise to the Black Muslims:

The need to affirm the goodness of creation was so strong that some black religious groups have done this at the expense of rejecting a doctrine of last things altogether. The pie in the sky futuristic hope of heaven has been totally abandoned in favor of a "this worldly" realized eschatology. If I understand the black Muslims fully on this point, they represent this type of reaction. If there be an objection that the black Muslims are not Christian, but Muslim, my reply will be that they do not belong to Classic Islam either. This sect, despite its borrowings from Islam, is more of a Christian heresy than it is a genuine sect a worldwide Islam. Furthermore, many of the same marks of oppression that have given birth to black theology gave rise to Black Muslims also.[75]

What Professor Roberts is stating is that due to the concept of "consciousness of kind" as pointed out by C. Eric Lincoln, the black Muslims have more in common with black theology than they do with classical Islam. A great percentage of black Christians began to view themselves as having more commonality with the rhetoric of black Muslims championing black liberation than many White Christians championing American exceptionalism. This is what many white Christians have difficulty understanding because they do not have the same shared experiences. They understood why black clergy would support the 1997 Promise Keepers movement's rally in Washington DC, led by white fundamentalists seeking to amplify the need for "coming together" of men across racial lines but did not understand why black Christians would support the Million Man March led by Louis Farrakhan in 1994. They were shocked by photos taken together by The Rev. Dr. Jeremiah Wright (Barack Obama's pastor in the early days of his presidential campaign) and Louis Farrakhan. Dr. Wright's sermons were and are strikingly like the rhetoric of Malcolm X and Louis Farrakhan.

When it was learned that Jeremiah Wright was the pastor of presidential aspirant and eventual president, Barack Obama, white Christian America was shaken and startled. This discovery arose out

---

[75] Roberts, Deotis J. *Liberation and Reconciliation.(* Maryknoll NY: Orbis Books, 1994), 42

of an opposition research video of Pastor Wright's sermon where he condemned America in the strongest terms, stating "God Damn America" for its history of cruelty and barbarism. The release of the video was designed to paint then senator Obama as too radical and unpatriotic for the White House. However, many black preachers came to Wright's and Obama's defense, stating that Wright's words were not unusual or uncommon in the black prophetic tradition. Given the insightful nature of Wright's sacred rhetoric, while revisiting America's unjust history, it is worthy of being quoted at length:

We confuse government and God. Let me tell you something; we believe in this country, and we teach our children that God sent us to this "Promised Land". He sent us to take this country from the Arrowak, the Susquehanna, the Apache, the Comanche, the Cherokee, the Seminole, the Choctaw, the Hopi and the Arapaho. We confuse Government and God. We believe God sanctioned the rape and robbery of an entire continent. We believe God ordained African slavery. We believe God makes Europeans superior to Africans and superior to everybody else too...We said in our founding document as a government, 'We hold these truths to be self-evident, that all men are created equal' – created, that means God – 'and endowed with a certain inalienable right' – that means given by God, and then we define Africans in those same documents as three-fifths of a person. We believe God approved of African slavery...

She put them in chains. The government put them in slave

quarters, put them on auction blocks, put them in cotton fields, put them in inferior schools, put them in substandard housing, put them in scientific experiments, put them in the lowest paying jobs, put them outside the equal protection of the law, kept them out of their racist bastions of higher education and locked them into position of hopelessness and helplessness. The government gives them the drugs, builds bigger prisons, passes a three-strike law, and then wants us to sing "God Bless America." No, no, no. Not "God Bless America"; God Damn America! That's in the Bible, for killing innocent people. God Damn America for treating her citizens as less than human. God Damn America as long as she keeps trying to act like she is God, and she is supreme! [76]

Reaction from the news media and American public to the radically prophetic lines in Jeremiah Wright's sermon proved the case that he made. What Wright made clear in his sermon is that America has been historically drunk from the wine of its own self-deception concerning its place in the world.

Believing that both her founding and presence in the world are divinely sanctioned and that all who have suffered at her hands were only paying the price for existing under the realm of her goodness. Therefore, Wright concluded that America sees itself as above criticism, unconsciously believing she is God. This false sense of American sacredness among White Americans which were exposed

---

[76] https://www.blackpast.org/african-american-history/2008-rev-jeremiah-wright-confusing-god-and-government/

by Wright is comparable to Dr. King's words in his famous Drum Major Instinct sermon when he remembered, *"not too long ago, a man down in Mississippi said that God was a charter member of the White Citizens Council. And so God being the charter member means that everybody who's in that has a kind of divinity, a kind of superiority."*[77]

Wright alleges that the American perspective is that whatever brutality and barbarism America exercises in the world, her belief in her own goodness erases it all. In this view, God's calling and establishing America, grants license to do what other nations are not allowed. Wright referred to the belief that America is the "Promised Land," and that God ordained the subjugation of its original nations and the institution of the enslavement of blacks for a higher purpose.

Wright brought attention to the White evangelical belief in God's close association with America and how any push back against this narrative is considered unpatriotic and hating America. If any other nation conducted itself as America has in its history, undoubtedly, they would criticize that nation along the same lines as Wright criticized America. If these same atrocities that Wright outlined were committed against White America by another nation, certainly they would also speak damnation against that nation, yet Wright's denunciations were considered blasphemous and profane to be spoken against a nation which considers itself to be sacred and God

---

[77] Martin Luther King Jr., Drum Major Instinct Sermon. Ebenezer Baptist Church, Atlanta Georgia, February 4, 1968.

ordained.

America is also aware that blacks and Native Americans have not forgotten the historical crimes that have been committed against them. Therefore, to maintain the sanitized and sacred view of America, it is preferable to the majority culture that these groups express loyalty and remain silent. To speak out in the way that Reverend Wright did, is considered ungrateful, because despite what they have experienced, in White America's view, they are living in what is considered God's country. The majority population is aware that black people and Native Americans may have such sentiments among them and therefore to be welcomed in the political arena, they must go overboard to show themselves as patriotic and committed to the belief in America's goodness. Wright, through his rhetoric, defied this arrangement. C. Eric Lincoln's analysis will show why the White American public were so horrified by Wright's rhetoric, and the reasons why so many black church goers did not relate to the shock which they felt. Upon hearing the words of Wright, white evangelicals immediately sought to draw a contrast by demanding and displaying pride of the country. What many white evangelicals miss, is the depth of the concerns for racism and injustice in black organizations. Notice how Lincoln describes the discomfort White America has when challenged on such issues.

Race has played a very important role in the lives of black people and in the history of black institutions. Assessment of the racial factors of positive and negative ought not be avoided. For example, when confronted by the radical and particularistic demands of the phenomenon like black liberation theology, many white Christians including theologians have quickly hoisted the flag of a universal Christendom as Brothers and Sisters in Christ while trying to escape responsibility for the contemporary pain and suffering inflicted upon black people. Similarly, some black Christians including pastors have felt uncomfortable in dealing with their racial past and present and will prefer to assert the universalism of the Gospel as an alternative to confronting the nettlesome problems of Christian racialism.[78]

Obama, having been a long-time member of the Trinity United Church, pastored by Jeremiah Wright, had his patriotism and belief in America's goodness called into question. What White America failed to realize is that within the black preaching tradition, there is the prophetic notion that our loyalty to God and His heavenly values are more important than love of country. The task of the prophet was not to flatter the nations, but rather to rebuke and correct them. So, in their reaction to the Wright sermon clip declaring "God damn America," proved his point that in their minds, they considered God and America are one and the same. What was lost in the interplay was that Jeremiah Wright's view was consistent with that of Dr. King and Malcolm X who considered themselves as Americans but were able to separate God's goodness and sovereignty from America's existence.

---

[78] Lincoln C. Eric, *The Black Church in African American Experience.* (Durham, NC: Duke University Press, 1990), 13

Malcolm X was considered the greatest of the two evils because he came across as being more of an expression of the anger and the rage which existed in the hearts and in the communities of Black America. Many fail to see that there exists an undercurrent within the black religious world that is upheld by consciousness of kind and may correctly be labeled black religion. In this sense, Jeremiah Wright and Malcolm X are part of the same religion which was expressed in similar ways. Professor J. Deotis Roberts states that this religion includes both the saints and sages of the black community. The reason why so many on the outside are unable to relate, is their unwillingness to consider or study the topics of interest among black people. Neglecting the study of black religion, black thought and black theology by the majority culture is the cause of the disconnect. This is true, while according to Roberts, a vast amount of material exists to gain an understanding and appreciation of the phenomena. In Roberts view, one cannot understand the black experience without comprehending black religion.[79]

What is black religion exactly? Professor Dwight Hopkins, a noted figure and author in the field of black liberation theology, defines it in the following terms:

Poor black folk created their own faith in the hell of over two-hundred years of slavery...From the seventeenth to nineteenth century, African and African American enslaved workers constructed a new religion drawing on three sources— memories of

---

[79] Roberts, Deotis J. *Liberation and Reconciliation.* Maryknoll NY: Orbis Books, 1994), 4

African religious beliefs, commonsense wisdom from everyday life, and a reinterpretation of the white supremacy Christianity introduced to them by their Christian slave masters.[80]

Jeremiah Wright's condemnation of a "Christian" America, which believed it was ordained of God, was consistent with the history of black religion. The "God Damn America" sentiment expressed by Jeremiah Wright is consistent with the speeches and rhetoric of Malcolm X and private in-house rhetoric of King. Jeremiah Wright explained in his sermon why he used the word "damn" by declaring "that's in the Bible." Jesus, according to the gospel, said that those who do not believe in the power of his love is condemned (which means to be damned) already. Although this word was used by Jesus himself, it was too harsh to be expressed against a nation which believed unequivocally in its own sacredness.

To prove his belief in America's goodness, Obama was politically required to humble himself as a black man and publicly denounce Wright and the church. Obama's denunciation of Wright came about after Obama initially defended him, stating that Wright is simply an older man who was still stuck in the Civil Rights era.

However, in subsequent interviews, Wright did not back down from his statements, therefore Obama was forced by his handlers to completely sever his connection from his pastor. When Obama made it to the White House, he made a statement to Black America

---

[80] Hopkins, Dwight L. *Introducing Black Theology of Liberation.* Maryknoll, New York: Orbis Books, 2014), 17

and its voters by regularly attending black churches on Sundays in Washington DC. Although he was required to politically cater to White America, he wanted it to be known that he was still rooted in the black community. White evangelical Americans hold the view that they have been on the right side of history from its inception, but historically speaking, the enslaved ancestors of black people viewed America as "Egypt Land." Therefore, the black religion takes a different position than the majority culture. Professor Roberts holds the view that Black historians and black theologians do not commonly view Nat Turner, the leader of the 1831 slave insurrection, as being on the wrong side of history as others might. Both Nat Turner and Fredrick Douglass were on God's side of history, from the perspective of black religion. Therefore, Professor Roberts places Nat Turner and Bonhoeffer together as persons who exhibited righteous anger to alleviate oppression and bring about justice for millions. One fought against Hitler and the other on behalf of the enslaved. Malcolm X and Jeremiah Wright represented that righteous anger which was historically expressed by those on the right side of history.

Michael Eric Dyson reveals the sensitivity that White society has toward the least hint of black anger, much less the provocative voices such as Wright. Dyson says as much in describing his own history in dealing with white audiences:

I knew that honest dialogue might rattle a white world that was not used to hearing a black man like me speak directly about race. No, my crime was far more mundane, I had whispered a prayer into a microphone in chapel during a Black History Month service asking God to help defeat racism in our midst. My few words set the white community on edge. My prayer was the clue that I wasn't mesmerized by the fictions of whiteness, that I wasn't satisfied with the sanctuary it wanted to provide. It was enough to tip off the president that I was ready for the revolution and that I was prepared to bring it on violently.[81]

What Dyson shows is that wherever black discontent or anger is expressed, there is the fear that some violent revolution is around the corner. Anger among European descendants toward its government is always justified, but is considered irreverent and disrespectful when expressed by black people.

One of the areas where Black Muslims resonated with the community was that white eschatological views made them unaccountable for racism. Consequently, many black theologians and clergy, as a social and psychological reaction, chose to focus on the present "hell" that black people were suffering at the hands of America and the need for a sociological salvation today. "Hell" as defined in liberation theology is much more than an eschatological destination but a present existential situation. Considering this view, professor J. Deotis Roberts, a critic of Cone--patriarch of black liberation theology, places Cone in the same vein as black Muslims who reject the afterlife as a reaction to oppression.[82]

---

[81] Dyson, 61.
[82] Roberts, 86.

Yet much more can be said of the motivation of White clergy in overemphasizing the afterlife in the presence of black people, which is highly self-serving. Such overemphasis has a dark undertone as it has been historically utilized to delay justice for millions. Despite his critique, Professor Roberts makes clear his position as it relates to black Christian theology and black power: *I stand somewhere between the generations that is on the boundary between the black militants and the old-fashioned civil rights integration and also between the by whatever means necessary emphasis and the view that ends and means are organically one.*[83]

While Roberts, placed himself on the boundary lines of black militancy and the traditional church-based struggle, Professor Cone, the father of black theology, placed himself clearly on the side of Malcolm X and black power. He explains how Dr. King and his associates delivered the black church from the complacency of a white theology of gradualism, but they did not deliver them from the White value system. Enslavement to this white value system, according to Cone, blinded them to the need to challenge those misplaced values instead of imitating them. Thus, they lost their unique and distinguishing identity. Consequently, the black church had become an imitation of the white churches their forefathers left. Additionally, Cone pushed back on the charge of heresy, by laying the charge squarely at the feet of the white church which either promoted or remained silent on racism. Cone says that he too was a

---

[83] Ibid, 1

part of the complacency that existed in the middle-class black church and credits Malcolm X and black power advocates for his spiritual and theological awakening when he says the following:

African Americans, it seemed to me at the time, had assumed that there was nothing wrong with whites thinking about God. It was the challenging and angry voice of Malcolm X that shook me out of my theological complacency. 'Christianity is the white man's religion,' he proclaimed again and again as he urged African Americans to adopt a perspective on God that would derive from their cultural history. [84]

Cone's theological awakening is an illustration of the powerful influence that Malcolm X and by extension, that black power exerted upon black theologians and Christians. Black Christians needed someone from outside the black church tradition to awaken them to their history and a sense of unapologetic racial dignity, because those who were on the inside were asleep to the realities of American Christianity. Malcolm X, to a great degree was what the black church needed to reconnect with the righteous anger and love of their own race.

Esau McCaulley, who is a professor of New Testament at Wheaton College and theologian in residence at Progressive Baptist Church, a historically Black congregation in Chicago, also

---

[84] *Cone, James H. and Lawrence H. Mamiya. Black Theology and Black Power.* (Maryknoll, New York: Orbis Books, 2018), 24

acknowledges the influence of Malcolm X in his own theological thought and expression. McCaulley references the movie "Malcolm X," which was played by Denzel Washington, and which premiered while he was a 7th grader, as being a spark for his interest in black pride and African heritage. In a time when the crack epidemic had spread throughout urban centers, the negative stereotypes of black youth by conservative politicians, a revival of Malcolm's vision for black America was on the rebound.

McCaulley observed that socially conscious hip-hop and anti-gang messages rose to prominence as a reaction to what was viewed as disrespect of the community. Furthermore, McCaulley draws our attention to the influence of the Nation of Islam and by default, other black consciousness groups have held with the black church.

Many in the Nation of Islam or other black consciousness groups criticize black Christians for following a religion that does so little for us. Black members of other religions or black secularists who critique Christianity because of this lack of concern for justice has followed black Christians since the beginning. This is a part of the two-sided critique that the black pastor has to deal with... not only must we push back on the European destruction of the Christian faith, but we must also take seriously the claims coming from black critics.[85]

Dwight Hopkins, a widely respected figure in the black theology movement, and professor at the Divinity School of the University of

---

[85] McCaulley, Esau. Reading While Black. Westmont, Illinois: Intervarsity Press, 2020), 75

Chicago, agrees with McCaulley as he describes Malcolm X as the premiere figure from the late 1950's and 60's who raised the awareness of the problems of black self-hatred. Malcolm, like a master psychologist, brought clarity to the damage inflicted through subconscious black inferiority. Malcolm was prominent among those who trumpeted throughout America that whiteness is not the standard for all that is good, beautiful, normal and right in the world. Hopkins points to Malcolm's speeches which were delivered with passion and conviction, explaining that blackness was sacred and not the equivalent of nastiness, ugliness and evil. That whiteness should never be considered the equivalent to cleanliness and moral uprightness, Malcolm trumpeted in public debates, interviews, and platforms in urban communities. Hopkins describes Malcolm as the one who shattered the myths of white superiority and black inferiority. Hopkins described Malcolm as a Hebrew scriptural prophet who wielded the flames of truth against principalities and powers, and as the singular figure of his time who trumpeted black solidarity, Pan-Africanism, black pride and black self-determination.

While politically, Malcolm preached black nationalism, theologically, according to Hopkins, he preached that the "white man is the devil." This was the catalyst, as Hopkins asserts, that sparked the black power movement and, in some cases, urban rebellions. From this, as the theory goes, the church was forced to decide whether to embrace or reject black cultural pride and solidarity. Black theology legitimized the affirmation of black humanity within the black church context. Hopkins further asserts that because the Civil Rights Freedom Movement had shifted in the direction of black power, the church found itself at a crossroads. They could either meet the people in their present reality or cling to the past to appease white liberals.

Many black theologians, according to Hopkins, and a vast proportion within the church, began to see the theological correctness in the slogan 'I'm black and I'm Proud.' This pride was different from that of victimizers and oppressors, who refuse to affirm the goodness of others, but one that asserts a God given dignity that had historically been denied. These theologians began to see that a correct and relevant theology addresses the problems of inequitable political, economic and cultural power. Indeed, this concept of black power was not outside of the gospel, but essential to it. Hopkins drew this theological conclusion concerning black theology and black power:

White Christians monopolize power without conscience while blacks had conscience but no power... the voices and protests of black people forced the issue of the role of Christianity in the African American community. Thus, black theology arose to affirm African American humanity and as an answer to the reality of Black liberation moving against white racism.[86]

Power within this context of self-affirmation is not the equivalent to White power, which is dehumanizing to non-Whites, but

---

[86] Hopkins, 33-35

represents the demand for the freedom to exercise one's God given prerogatives, abilities and gifts, which had been hindered, along with equal access to Earth's resources, such as wealth and land.

Black theologian and Morehouse graduate, Raphael Warnock, who presently serves as pastor of the historic Ebenezer Baptist Church in Atlanta, agrees with Hopkins and McCaulley on the influence of "Muslim cleric" Malcolm X on black theologians. Warnock also serves as the first black Senator from Georgia. He argues the following:

It was nascent black theologians conscientized by the activist ministry of Martin King, challenged by the critique of King by the Muslim cleric Malcolm X and a young black power activist whom he had politically influenced, informed by the claims about rising black consciousness and led primarily by the constructive theological work of James Cone, who would begin to develop a self-conscious and systematic understanding of the black church as an instrument of liberation, and this mission...demanded a radical separation from the theological assumptions of white Christianity.[87]

Like J. Deotis Roberts, who stated that his theological journey lies on the crossroads between the traditional civil rights movement and that of Black solidarity, this is also true of the black church, according to Warnock. Warnock suggests that both movements (black power and traditional civil rights) have had a dramatic impact on the church, and that the church continues to seek understanding

---

[87] Warnock, Raphael. Divided Mind of the Black Church. New York: NYU Press, 2013), 39

on how to fully embrace the idea of black power. Warnock introduces the idea that the development of black theology as a discipline may be far ahead of where the church presently positions itself today.

The radical implications of these two movements have clearly been formative for the development of black theology as an intellectual discipline. However, what is not altogether clear is the extent to which the black church has fully integrated the theological meaning of black power and the epoch-making implications of King's ministry into its very self-understanding nearly two generations after his death.[88]

Migration and Assimilation

During the time of the Great Migration from Southern plantations to the large cities of the Midwest and East Coast, there existed side by side with the introduction to socially conscious black religion, promoted by Black Moors and Black nationalist street preachers promoting self-determination and black pride, and Black middle-class church goers. Alternative religions outside of the black church and the socially conscious movements were foremost in deconstructing white ideas concerning religion and culture. Whether they were a part of the church or not, black thought in the Northern cities were a product of black slave religion.

Professor James Cone shares with his readers that the most

---

[88] Ibid, 12

visible group which responded to the evils of white supremacy and the need to understand the sacredness of blackness was the Nation of Islam. Admitting that this form of black thought was the lens through which he made his own theological case, Professor Cone states the following:

Although many blacks rejected the claims of Christianity, they did not reject religion... The most visible group of this persuasion is the Nation of Islam often called the black Muslims in response to white people's oppression of blacks. They concluded that the white man is the devil whose destruction is inevitable at the hands of Allah. The black Muslims expound an ideology that equates Blackness with good and whiteness with evil, thereby fostering the belief that black people be completely self-determining despite white oppression. [89]

Cone embraced Malcolm's idea that black people should not wait until full integration was achieved to be socially uplifted and that it was indeed possible whether integration or reconciliation were achieved or not. Black people, whether they were welcomed into the mainstream of society or not, were fully capable of rising to greatness on its own terms through its own institutions.

Within the context of the Northern migrations, many churches that had been well established there for generations, middle class blacks began to embrace the idea that slave religion was backward and that to truly integrate they had to also assimilate. They believed that once they gained respectability by rejecting the ways of their

---

[89] Cone, James H. *God of the Oppressed.* Maryknoll, New York: (Orbis Books, 1997), 275

ancestors, they would move closer to integration and freedom. Therefore, many churches in the North shunned religious practices and exercises that reminded them of the ways of the past when slaves worshiped on the plantations and hush harbors. For example, they sought to move away from Negro spirituals, hand clapping, shouting, raising of hands and other emotional displays. These would be viewed as shameful and uncivilized compared to the White world, in their opinion, in which they were trying to assimilate. They pushed for education and a more sophisticated manner of worship. Dancing was shunned because it reminded them of Africa and what they saw as their shameful past. Simultaneously the black nationalist and the black Muslims were teaching on the streets that black people should be proud of themselves and their African heritage.

Black street preachers in the North believed that black people should not concern themselves too much with integration and assimilation, but a love of self and a rejection of whiteness. As a result of these assimilationist attitudes, the churches of the North and the Midwest noticed a decline in support and attendance. Consequently, because of these attitudes, they saw themselves as losing out and losing followers to the black Muslims, the black nationalists and other social and conscious groups. It was then that they began to question and re-examine their positions and began to embrace an attitude that perhaps they had much of which to be proud. There were those who began to see that they should not look at the white world as the standard for what was normal and acceptable. Since these new attitudes began to develop, churches began to adopt more of a black centered way of worshiping and interpreting scripture in terms of being unashamedly black and unapologetically Christian. Additionally, they began to view church less as a venue for social validation but spiritual formation in the black tradition.[90]

The Trinity United Church in Chicago that was famously pastored by the reverend Jeremiah Wright is a prime example of the influence of the black nationalists, socially conscious movements and the black Muslims. They saw that churches could no longer afford to embrace Eurocentric ideals nor could they accept that black centered ways of thinking and worshiping were backward or unrefined. To keep up with the moods and the attitudes of the black community, they were then forced to take a second look at what it meant to be both black proudly so and Christian. They began to teach more about the history of black people as they began to criticize the prejudice and discrimination as exercised by the larger White Society. Critiquing the government and those who are in leadership and the white power structure, they began to embrace more so the religion of the ancestors. Hand-clapping returned, along with drums and hand waving. Shouting was again normalized and the idea that one could be a middle class black and simultaneously engaged in charismatic worship practices.

Sociologist and chairman of the department of sociology at

---

[90] Speller, Julia Michelle. Unashamedly Black and unapologetically Christian: One congregation's quest for meaning and belonging (PhD thesis). The University of Chicago. p. 2005

Catholic University of America and historian Anne Kusener Nelson wrote on the movement of black people from the south and the desire for assimilation in pursuit of full integration. Integration meant that black people could no longer be excluded from the same resources that were accessible to Whites, but assimilation meant imitating the ways and values of the larger society to gain acceptability. Assimilation required that black people bury much of their culture in order to overcome negative stereotypes and make whites comfortable with them. According to the Nelsons, this was particularly true of the black church after the great migration, and this created an opening for black consciousness groups in the North.

Additionally, the authors acknowledge that this was especially true of middle-class blacks, who anticipated the day when they would be embraced by white society. They did not want to appear undignified in any sense to the white world. Such attitudes among such black people caused them to look down on those who did not appear as distinguished as they were, which brought about black classism. The authors clearly exposed the problematic nature of this mentality.

As real integration seems imminent, the black middle class removed or attempted to remove identifying names from their church organizations such as the words colored or African. Furthermore, there was a tendency to move away from the more traditional black denominations into the Presbyterian, congregational and Episcopal churches. Frazier seems to believe that with the increasing assimilation it could not survive as a spiritual and social refuge for blacks of any class.[91]

Why the removal of all things with the words African or Colored? Black people in Africa are proudly a part of the "Anglican" church, but black people in America wanted to move away from the label "African." This subtle and unconscious inferiority needed to be exposed. It was because Africa was viewed by the white world as savage, beastly and backward, that this thinking emerged. Since whiteness was the standard of dignity, they sought to disassociate themselves with the term "colored," in their organizational names. Simultaneously, black pride groups were emerging that became exceptionally attractive to both those in the ghettos and in some cases the middle-class. The black church had not yet anticipated the shift in black consciousness. Churches such as the Jeremiah Wright's Trinity United Church of Christ in Chicago and Albert Cleage's Shrine of the Black Madonna in Detroit were responses to this shift.[92]

What many black professionals also did not anticipate is that with every forward movement toward integration, white resentment would follow. However, white backlash to black progress in the age of integration and urban protest has to a great degree saved the black church from complete assimilation into Euro American thought and value systems. Illusions of a future with a colorless identity, in many

[91] Nelson, Hart M.; Anne Kusener Nelson (1975). Black Church in the 1960s. Lexington, KY: (University Press of Kentucky, 2014), 8-9
[92] Ibid, 8-9

ways drove many black churchpersons and traditional civil rights groups in their resistance to the language of black power and Pan-Africanism. They had incorrectly confused integration with liberation. Liberation required political, cultural and economic power. Integration was part of the process; it was a means to an end. The message of integration was not a demand to assimilate, but a moral political action which stated, according to the philosophy of Kwame Ture, that no society that benefits from what we have built will tell us where we can or cannot exist, nor will any be allowed to define or limit our rights as human beings. It was black power that added the dimension drove the vision that we will exist in the full expression of our culture, black humanity and value system with full access to America's resources for empowerment and opportunity." Kwame Ture (formerly Stokely Carmichael) identified the sociological and psychological reasons why there was so much backlash to the idea of black power by the NAACP and other churchpersons in their quest for integration. His thoughts were printed in his autobiography entitled "Ready for Revolution." In his own words he and his fellow SNCC scholars, after much research, concluded that *"the unspoken, unexamined, and unacceptable assumption of the "integration" being preached was that nothing of value or permanence could be created by black people in association with themselves."* Ture further adds that the pushback was due to the fear that if we are too black in our rhetoric, this somehow will interfere with our assimilation/integration model, and consequently all efforts toward integration would be lost. Notice his words:

The American 'melting pot' meant us—as a people—assimilating, despite racist resistance, the culture and values of the mainstream, hoping to pass over into and be 'accepted' by the white community on their terms, To blend in, call no attention to differences—in effect, to sneak into white acceptance. Clearly a form of cultural suicide. Then we said that the solution to our problems had nothing to do with our 'acceptance' by white America and less with 'universal brotherhood.' Our struggle had to be about power. [93]

This is the work in which Malcolm X and Ture were engaged, which was to pull black America away from the gulf of cultural suicide and to believe in themselves and their heritage. When the nation of Israel was founded outside of the borders of Egypt, the Torah was written, which created a distinct culture. Annual feasts, rituals and rites of passage were established so that their history would be remembered, and their culture would forever remain intact. Likewise, black America also miraculously developed a distinct culture and possessed a rich heritage. Those who were promoting self-determination and community empowerment were engaged in godly work for the salvation of black dignity. John writes in Revelation 7:9-12, that all languages nations and cultures will have a place in the new kingdom. Though challenged by those who

---

[93] Carmichael, Stokely and Thelwell, Ekweuemene Michael. *Ready for Revolution—The Life and Struggle of Stokely* Carmichael (Kwame Ture.) New York, New York: (Shribner, 2003), 531

had faith in assimilation and respectability politics, their advocacy began to resonate among the black populace.

Respectability politics, as the term is utilized today, was always in the background in the struggle for integration, and subsequently black power activists came along in the late 60s shined a light on this negative yet almost invisible sociological dynamic. The futility of respectability politics was exposed when Reverend Martin Luther King Jr. was shot and assassinated in Memphis, not in a dashiki, but in a suit and tie, in April of 69'. This resulted in the heightened awareness of the validity of black power, and the bad faith of the U.S. government supported by the mainstream.

The misinterpretation and mislabeling of black power advocacy by prominent black leaders such as Roy Wilkins, were done for the purpose of soothing white fears about black violence and retribution, and to distance themselves from rhetoric they believed would make white liberals and the American media feel uncomfortable enough to reject integration. Ture makes clear that black power language did not include anything inflammatory or revolutionary but was merely a continuation of historical rhetoric that began as soon as Africans landed on American shores. From that time until now, Ture explains, liberation was never about simply being among "white folks,' but the refusal and rejection of any arbitrary limits imposed on us by American apartheid. He states that too many confused their opposition to apartheid/segregation and second-class status, to being in favor of the white liberal's vision for integration. Ture defined black power as nothing as outrageous as overthrowing America and ruling over white people, as some pretended to fear, but simply about asserting our humanity as equal members of the human family of nations. When countering the sociological and political dynamics by civil rights leaders who vociferously denounced black power as reverse racism, he concludes the following:

[It was] simply about the power to affirm our black humanity; to defend the dignity, integrity, and institutions of our culture; and to collectively organize the political and economic power, to begin to control and develop our communities...Our goal and direction could not be about deserting our communities as refugees to white suburbia, but toward controlling, and developing our own communities. Not about abandoning our culture and rich heritage in order to 'integrate' into an American mainstream, then, as now, self-consciously defined as culturally 'white' and Eurocentric. [94]

Ture, in referencing the difficulties of achieve the goals of political, cultural and economic power, admitted that the answers are not easy. He goes on to utilize theological language he had heard from many preachers who associated the black struggle with the exilic language of scripture. He acknowledged that *"the devil was in the details on how to develop the unity and the strategies to make this possible in a strange land? And in the face of the pervasive white media manipulation."* [95]

Ture further adds, in answering black critics in the civil rights establishment, that black power was not only political but also

[94] Ibid, 531
[95] Ibid, 531

cultural, which was to be fulfill the need to *consciously and publicly free ourselves from the heritage of demeaning definitions and limitations imposed on us over centuries of colonial conditioning by a racist culture. Cultural and psychological self-determinations, that's all...if this was the discussion that this torrent of disinformation and intimidation was intended to derail, then I had some real bad news for them. They were way too late...This discussion—however suppressed—had long been underway among our people...the train has already left the station.* [96]

Quite frequently, whenever black people seek to express the importance of their role in history, the sacredness of their humanity and faith in themselves, there will be those who decry that "black supremacy is just as bad as white supremacy. This was the case among many NAACP supporters in the early days of black power and exists today among many black political conservatives and many well-intentioned ones who are concerned about hurting those in the predominant society. If somehow, a black leader or spokesperson in seeking to express the value of black humanity, says an intemperate word to some degree, it is not the same as white supremacy. Extreme rhetoric on the part of some black people who are seeking to make their claim as members of the human family is a reaction to the pain that centuries of enslavement, colonialism, chain gangs, Jim Crowism and mass incarceration that white supremacy has caused. It can never be the equivalent, because black

---

[96] Ibid, 527

people are only attempting to declare their place in history as equal contributors to civilization and humankind. One response represents fighting for their group's humanity, while the other has historically and continues to demean the group's humanity. Black power represented that fight for group humanity.

The NAACP and those who unwittingly were hoping for assimilation and colorlessness, needed the critique that people such as Malcolm and Ture were giving. They along with the masses needed to de-center whiteness and recenter blackness in the quest for freedom. Their limited imagination did not allow for this. What was needed may be found in one account that Ture gives concerning a black heckler at one of the street preaching events in Harlem. In the encounter, the male heckler, whose hair was permed, or as Ture described "freshly fried." The heckler shouted "I will never trade my Cadillac for an Elephant" as the preacher began to speak about the pride of African heritage and liberation. The "freshly fried" haired gentleman continued to demean and mock Africa's rich history. The speaker began to illustrate something that was quite instructive for those who were advancing colorlessness and respectability politics then and now. The speaker admonished the audience, *"pay no attention to this heckler, (and utilizing the language of the black church in illustrating those whom Jesus sought to deliver) this man is deaf, dumb, and blind,"* while simultaneously touching his eyes, ears and mouth. Teaching and illustrating, the speaker added another acted metaphor as he held out his hands and gestured as if it were about to drizzle, and mockingly stated that *"this man's hair will return back to Africa before his mind does."* [97]Roars and laughter followed, but the point was made; many black people in America were racist against themselves due to miseducation. Healing meant dismantling Eurocentric indoctrination and erecting black centered philosophical paradigms on a psychological level. Part of the liberating work of God is to unmute the mouth (help the silent ones to have the courage to speak for themselves and community,) unstop the ears (help them hear the needs of their community and the plots of those working against them,) and open the eyes (understand their plight, their value and noble history) of the miseducated black leader and laity through the true history of black self-determination and African heritage.

What the socially conscious--Nas (Nasir Jones) rapped about in the lyrics of his 2003 hit song "I Can," is what Malcolm, Garvey, the Harlem Street preachers, and eventually Kwame Ture were offering black America when he stated the following:

Be, be, 'fore we came to this country

We were kings and queens, never porch monkeys

There was empires in Africa called Kush

Timbuktu, where every race came to get books

To learn from black teachers who taught Greeks and Romans

Asians and Arabs who gave them gold when

Gold was converted to money it all changed

Money then became empowerment for Europeans

---

[97] Ibid, 101

Be, B-boys and girls, listen up

You can be anything in the world, in God we trust.[98]

This was the message of Dr. King in his "black is beautiful" proclamation, which is the affirmation that we are free to be ourselves in American society and have every reason to be proud. Our greatness was intact millennia before we encountered the European, therefore our present and future greatness does not depend upon white acceptance, but upon the uninhibited exercise of our full humanity. We will receive full respect in the world community because we chose to demand it.

Demand for respect by the larger society in all our blackness, regardless of white acceptance, was the focus of black power. We demand to be respected, not based on their understanding of what it means, but as we understand it. We do not need to earn it; it is owed to us as bearers of God's own image. We had dignity, freedom and a history of accomplishment before we came to the shores of America in chains, without assimilation. Liberation is about restoration not only to what we were, but our potential as Nasir Jones rapped, *"before it all changed...when gold was converted into money for the empowerment of Europeans."*

Assimilation would be an insult to our ancestors, whose humanity did not rely on the white embrace. Integration was not about getting White's to embrace blacks, but blacks demanding

---

98 https://genius.com/Nas-i-can-lyrics

equal participation in a world they built. The Roy Wilkins types along with the masses in the North and South needed this liberating work, so that they might be re-educated about their own power as human beings, and their right to demand equality rather than beg for acceptance. It appeared as if they were willing to take whatever crumbs were thrown at them just to be embraced. This was the challenge that confronted Ture and his associates. Malcolm commanded the most attention in this liberating work, and Ture and other militants would follow in his footsteps. It was understood that our minds needed liberated to properly understand who we were and where we needed to go.

These convictions and beliefs, influenced by the Harlem Renaissance and speeches of Malcolm X, that would later draw the attention of Malcolm's early mentor and leader of the Nation of Islam—Elijah Muhammad. Muhammad invited Ture (then Carmichael) and leaders of SNCC to his Chicago campus and residence in Chicago in 1966. Ture was impressed and amazed that such a frail, mannerly and soft- spoken gentleman, could rise from such impoverished conditions on a dirt farm in Georgia, and command such a dynamic and loyal following which numbered in the thousands. He appreciated the work that Muhammad accomplished on the street-level for black people, and his vision for the development of black institutions, but could not envision the NOI and the SNCC organizations working together due to its negative history surrounding Malcolm X and its strict philosophical dynamics. Additionally, Ture and SNCC could not envision themselves as working closely with one who insisted so fervently on his own supposedly divinely given messianic role within Black America (This was large bulk of their conversation in the meeting.) Blacks would gain their freedom through divine intervention, was Muhammad's position, which did not square with SNCC activism. Ture says that the *visit simply confirmed our opinion that SNCC would have to try to build Black Power and advance our people's interest while avoiding narrow nationalist regimentation or religious fundamentalism.* [99]

Ture's autobiographical work cited Eric Ture Muhammad, who later acknowledged the oral history of the event within the NOI and how Elijah Muhammad instructed their security apparatus/Fruit of Islam to protect Kwame Ture (then Stokely Carmichael) *wherever he moves in the world.* Ture would later move to West Africa to continue his Pan-African work in the country of Guinea. This illustrates the connection between black religion and black power advocates of the 1960s. There is an invisible spiritual connection that exists among the various wings of the struggle throughout American history.

Black Jesus vs White Jesus

Womanist theologian, canon theologian of Washington National Cathedral, and dean of Episcopal Divinity School at Union Theological Seminary--Kelly Brown Douglas, addresses the

---

[99] Ture, 523

influence of Malcolm X on black theological expression. While there have been exceptions, such as Bishop Henry Neal Turner, in raising the issue of the black Deity, there was little evidence for such in the history of American black rhetoric, since Turner. Professor Cone refers to Bishop Turner, who in response to the psychological warfare against African humanity by many European-American Christians, went as far as proclaiming that God himself was a Negro. Cone described Bishop Turner's resistance in the following words:

Although Turner was elected bishop in the AME church, he was not the typical holder of that office. The more whites demeaned blackness as a mark of inferiority, the more Turner glorified it. At a time when black and white Christians identified God with European images and the AME Churches were debating whether to replace the word 'African' in their name with 'American,' Turner shocked everyone with his declaration that "God is a Negro."

Indeed, Bishop Turner was far ahead of his time, for such a theology had not grasped the attention of the black masses until the advent of Malcolm generations later.[100] Andre E. Johnson, a professor at Memphis Theological Seminary, and scholar concerning the history and rhetoric of Turner acknowledges the following:

By maintaining that all theology is at its core a form of argument,

---

[100] Cone, James. *Martin and Malcolm and America;* Maryknoll NY: (Orbis Books 1991), 25

"rhetorical theology" places emphasis on how a speaker or writer situates language in order to persuade its hearers to a certain position. In other words, when Turner spoke and wrote "God is a Negro," he was not doing systematic theology, he was engaged in a public theology - a rhetorical enterprise, that had as its aim a persuasive function within a specific context. [101]

As Douglas suggested, Malcolm's critique of whiteness and his declarations that Jesus was black, influenced a community which was felt by the black church and its theologians. Malcolm's power in urban America was too strong, and as Douglas would put it, "impossible" to resist. All black religious thinkers were forced to respond. Douglas further comments that while Malcolm was correct in raising the issue of Christ's color, unlike abolitionist Frederick Douglas, he missed the mark in not distinguishing between slaveholding Christianity of America as a tool for enslavement and black slave Christianity as a tool of resistance.

That King's embrace of non-violent resistance for equal rights was an example of the passivity of Christianity, was Malcolm's perspective, never mind the philosophy came from Mahatma Ghandi who embraced eastern spirituality. Douglas shares that Malcolm was correct in his assessment of the influence of Slaveholding Christianity upon too many among black Christians. King however, according to Douglas, made a clear distinction

---

[101] "God is a Negro: The (rhetorical) black theology of bishop Henry McNeal" by Andre E. Johnson (memphis.edu)

between the Jesus of southern whites and the true Jesus who stood up for the marginalized. Moreover, according to Douglas, King did not express an appreciation or the importance of Christ's color and the way he has been historically depicted. She declares that King did not observe how portrayals of Jesus as a white man in a white supremacist society affected black people on a psychological level. This was however, in Douglas' observation, where Malcolm hit his strongest note on his critique of black assimilation, black passivity and agreement with depictions of a white Jesus within the church.

Douglas highlights the issue by pointing out Malcolm's view that it was a form of oppression to have black people worshiping a God who resembled those who brutalized and dehumanized them. Douglas' shows how Malcolm made the connection between black passivity, black inferiority and the worship and admiration of a blonde haired blue-eyed pale skin God. Bringing attention to the black inferiority complex and admiration for whiteness among too many within the black church, Douglas connects black psychologist Kenneth Clarke's findings with the observations of Malcolm X:

Black psychologist Kenneth Clarke had already explained in his arguments before The United States Supreme Court during the 1954 Brown versus Board of Education case, how important it was for black people, particularly black children, to have positive black images. His research demonstrated that a bombardment of white images and symbols severely damages self-worth and self-esteem. Essentially Clarke's finding supported Malcolm X's observation that black worship of white images, even Christ, is unhealthy and reflective of black people's psychological and emotional enslavement to a white racist culture.[102]

It is quite remarkable that as early as 1895, prior to Garvey, Clarke, Elijah Muhammad and Malcolm, Bishop Turner understood the psychological damage of black inferiority programming. Stephen Ward Angell, who wrote extensively on Turner, provides a reference to his thinking on this topic when he writes the following as cited by John Dittmer in *Black Leaders of the Nineteenth Century,* Turner wrote in 1898: *"As long as we remain among the whites, the Negro will believe that the devil is black. . . that he [as a black person] is the devil... "* [103]. and the effect of such sentiment is contemptuous and degrading. These are the thoughts that Malcolm and eventually Martin King and black theologians echoed. There is nothing sacred about whiteness as a theory, and indeed black humanity reflects God himself. Cone points to the influence of Black Muslim theology in the area of God's blackness, within the larger religious community when he shows how *"in Black Muslim theology, the almighty black God is the source of all good and power, "* and in its attempt to explain the problem of evil and black suffering, mythologizes or envisions that a renegade scientist named Yacob, in rebellion against the Black Creator God, created the European race with evil intentions. According to this religious mythology, Yacob deliberately created Europeans in order to fill the

---

[102] Douglas, Kelly Brown. *The Black Christ.* New York: (Orbis Books, 2019), 88

[103] https://www.encyclopedia.com/people/history/us-history-biographies/henry-mcneal-turner

world with *liars and murderers,* by which black people have been victimized to date.[104] While this mythology fails to resonate with the majority of Black people, it is the background for Malcolm's view of the blackness of the Deity which helped in his personal healing and emancipation. Some may argue that racializing God as Black is irreverent and profane, because God is a Spirit who exists far above human conceptions of nationality and race. What is perhaps hypocritical about this notion is that such complaints or denunciations never came to the forefront over the long centuries where Deity was depicted as hoary headed white male, and angels as blonde haired and white. Such objections are nonexistent until those ideas are overturned in the minds of Black people. Professor Cone addresses this theological hypocrisy when he says

"The difficulty of white theologians in recognizing their racial interest in this issue can be understood only in the light of the social context of theological discourse. They cannot see the Christological validity of Christ's blackness because their axiological grid blinds them to the truth of the biblical story. For example, the same white theologians who laughingly dismiss Albert Cleage's 'Black Messiah' say almost nothing about the European (white) images of Christ plastered all over American homes and churches. I perhaps would respect the integrity of their objections to the Black Christ on scholarly grounds, if they applied the same vigorous logic to Christ's whiteness, especially in contexts where his blackness is not

---

[104] Cone, Martin, Malcolm and America, 27

advocated."[105]

It must be understood that the concepts of Deity as advocated by Turner and Muhammad would not exist if the ideas of white superiority and Deity were not merged. Turner and Muhammad's ideas were a tool of resistance in a world that was structured on the basis of black inferiority constructs. Additionally, Cone states that this is only one explanation in the following description:

"…many white critics of black theology question blackness as a Christological title, because it appears to be determined exclusively by the psychological and political needs of black people to relate theology to the emergence of black power in the later 1960s. That is only partly true. The phrase "Black Christ" refers to more than subjective states and political expedience of black people at a given point in history. Rather this title is derived primarily from Jesus' past identity, his present activity, and his future coming as each is dialectically related to the others…The 'blackness of Christ,' therefore is not simply a statement about skin color, but rather, the transcendent affirmation that God has not ever, no not ever, left the oppressed alone in struggle. He was with them in Pharaoh's Egypt, is with them in America, Africa and Latin America, and will come in the end of time to consummate fully their human freedom.[106]

Cone, in addressing the need for psychological healing among

---

[105] *Cone, God of the Oppressed, 203*
[106] Cone, God of the Oppressed, 203, 208

African descendants in America, said that both integrationists due to the influence of nationalists and nationalists themselves were fighting the *power of 'white over black' and its psychological impact upon the self-esteem of its victims.* The crosswinds of their public rhetoric had its impact whether the two camps realized it or not, was Cone's position. [107] This was particularly true as many black churches began to evolve and heal in this area, as so many are continuing to heal unto this day.

Kelly Brown Douglas makes an important contribution to black religious thought by illustrating the distinct and significant roles that both Martin and Malcolm played. According to Douglas, Martin carried the torch of a slave religion that never stopped resisting, while Malcolm's rhetoric served as a wakeup call for a black self-esteem connected to a black Jesus. Douglas concludes that the black church needs the combination of both, and that Christ himself, as a liberator, possessed the spirit of both. She adds the following concerning Malcolm and Martin.

If Martin and Malcolm did not make this clear, the demands from young black power advocates sometimes refer to as the angry children of Malcolm X certainly made it clear.[108]

Studying this history, Douglas suggests that the seeds of black dignity and a black Christ, sown by Malcolm, eventually bloomed within the late 80s and early 90s. Malcolm's influence, whether admitted or not, looms large within the modern Black Church.

---

[107] Cone, Malcom and Martin and America, 27, 28
[108] Kelly Brown Douglas, 88

Douglas states the following:

Some 30 years [from 1963] later, especially with the emergence of the Afrocentric movement in the black community, many black scholars and church leaders are vociferously repeating Malcolm's proclamation.[109]

What black clergy and theologians had to grasp, was that exclusion from the mainstream of American society was only part of the problem with black people. There was also the psychological trauma and the demonization of Africa and blackness that needed to be addressed. Black people needed more than integration; they needed to be healed from the mental disease of deferential treatment of all things white. Christ himself was a healer and would certainly exercise his healing grace that was needed to be cured from black inferiority. This healing could only occur by dismantling images that harm black dignity and being reminded that black people came from a legacy of greatness. Malcolm, although he was not a Christian, was doing the work of Jesus by diagnosing those psychological shackles and breaking them through his masterful teaching and rhetoric. He also did this work by bringing whiteness down from its image of innocence and moral uprightness to that of deviousness and exploitation. Because too many theologians and Christian leaders were not feeding this hunger nor providing for this thirst, those on the outside of the traditional civil rights movement found a ready audience. It was this reality that caused so many Christian leaders to

---

[109] Ibid, 24

recognize the need that had not previously been fulfilled. Douglas acknowledges this in her assessment of SNCC after the rise of black power advocacy:

If King and his Christian principles were not going to liberate black people from the physical and psychological bonds of white racism, then black power advocates were far more than willing to leave both King and Christianity behind. The young black students of SNCC in fact did this when they turned toward Malcolm X.[110]

It was the black students of SNCC, post-Malcolm assassination, that awakened black Christian leaders of a neglected aspect of black freedom and liberation, which was a restoration of black dignity. This meant correcting and dismantling the misinformed historical narratives created by the white American establishment which fed into the psychology of black inferiority. This would later lead to the embrace of Afrocentrism by the black church.

Weaponized Forgiveness

Another important contribution from Malcolm was the critique he made of the emphasis on forgiveness by White and Black Christians. Malcolm did not believe that forgiveness or redemption were wrong; he was a model forgiveness and second chances through his own personal story. There was something devious about those who had gained power through oppression demanding forgiveness to avoid accountability. Malcolm, unlike so many, was

---

[110] Ibid, 91-92

able to see through the charade. Forgiveness was being made a central theme because too many blacks did not want to do the hard work of demanding justice and repair, nor did they want to endure the discomfort of making white people uncomfortable. White people demanded forgiveness because they recognized that a great debt was owed to its black citizens which they were unwilling to pay. Thus, throughout American Christian history, forgiveness has been weaponized to avoid the necessary sacrifices to restore black dignity.

While non-violence was indeed an effective strategy by those who were involved in direct action campaigns of civil disobedience, the negative side-effect was the impression that black people were the only people on Earth who did not have the right to defend themselves against violence. This weaponization of forgiveness and non-violence, Malcolm X, and those who studied his speeches rejected. Forgiveness and non-violence do not need to be demanded by the oppressor to the oppressed, but rather it needs to be demanded by the oppressed who have for centuries been the victims of violence and white denial. Recognizing this truth presented by Malcolm and later black power activists, Professor and black liberation theologian, James Cone comments on the misplaced priorities when discussing forgiveness and non-violence.

Cone suggested that Whites should not be offended when black people discuss ways to defend themselves in the face of white violence and cruelty, nor should they be shocked when their calls for forgiveness remain unanswered. According to Cone, White

Christians are making a cruel gesture by reminding black people about the doctrine of reconciliation when they are the cause for the estrangement and alienation. He further comments that it is an act of hostility itself to demand forgiveness and reconciliation while the crimes are still being committed. Cone understands that such demands for reconciliation, love and forgiveness are abused for the sake of maintaining power in American society, and that the Jesus of liberation would never approve.

The difficulty is not with the reconciliation forgiveness question itself but with the people asking it. Like the question of violence. This question is almost always addressed to blacks by whites as if we blacks are responsible for the demarcation of community on the basis of color. They who are responsible for the dividing walls of hostility, racism and hatred want to know whether the victims are ready to forgive and forget without changing the balance of power. They want to know whether we have any hard feelings towards them, whether we still love them even though we are oppressed and brutalized by them.[111]

Cone was among the first black theologians who understood the unethical dynamic behind the weaponization and abuse of the concept of forgiveness as Malcolm X and black power advocates understood. For white Christians to demand that black people not hate them while simultaneously supporting or remaining silent while seeing their black neighbors being subject to hate, was the height of

---

[111] Cone, God of the Oppressed, 328

inhumanity. White Christians should have the courage to demand love from their own White neighbors so that the hateful crimes committed against blacks come to end. Cone, who was influenced by Malcolm, tackled the subject in a way that had never been addressed by any Christian theologian before him. Both Cone and Malcolm were expressing the sentiment that if White Christians reflected the love of Jesus themselves, instead of demanding it of black people, they would show it by being as angry as Malcolm and other blacks about the injustices committed against them. To empathize in this way is to connect with the words of James Baldwin who said, *"To be a Negro in this country and to be relatively conscious...is to be in a rage almost...all the time,* and to use the words of theologian, Claude Atcho,..That being conscious on an empathetic level is *"to feel the tremors of rage, lament and bewilderment due to [racism's] brutal assault on body and spirit [to the degree of] weeping, lamenting, shaking in anger for...the reality of hell on earth...for the devastating anticreational suffering that accompanies the sin of enslavement."* [112]

Black Economics

While most civil rights leaders of the 1960s emphasized equal rights under the Constitution and equal access to public accommodations and educational institutions. Malcolm X emphasized the need for independence from White Society and self-

---

[112] Atcho, Claude. *Reading Black Books.* Grand Rapids, Michigan: (Brazos Press, 2022), 113

reliance.

The black Muslims, particularly those based in Chicago, boasted of the myriad of black businesses that were created out of the encouragement and teaching of The Honorable Elijah Muhammad--the leader of the black Muslim movement. Malcolm and other Muslims picked up the mantle of Elijah Muhammad and began to teach throughout the Midwest and the East Coast, that in order for black people to gain their complete freedom, they should strive to no longer be dependent on the racist power structure for goods and services, but empower themselves economically through business initiatives and supporting one another for the flourishing of the race.

The idea was that by continuing to frequent white businesses and relying upon them for goods and services perpetuated the power that the white race has been holding over them for generations. The philosophy of Elijah Muhammad and Malcolm X said that black dollars should not leave the community to empower their oppressors.

The black Muslims believed that the total integration and assimilation economically by black people would in a sense extend their socioeconomic enslavement. Chicago was the headquarters for the black Muslim movement, which not only preached about community empowerment and freedom from the dependence on the white power structure, but they set the example for all of their followers by creating schools, universities, dry cleaners, laundry mats, grocery stores, restaurants, farms and banks. This would serve as an example of what all black Muslims and black people in general should practice.

Today churches within the black community, in the tradition of the Civil Rights Movement, continue to emphasize human rights as it relates to voting rights, prison reform, the militarization of the police and equal access to medical services. There is also a greater emphasis, since the 1960s Civil Rights Movement, on the need for black banks black businesses and strengthening historically black colleges and Universities. Supporting and growing black businesses has become a core value within a great number of black churches today. The push for human rights by the black church by appealing to the political system is the legacy of Martin Luther King Jr and other civil rights leaders.

Additionally, the appeal internally for the building of black businesses is largely the legacy of Malcolm X and the black Muslim movement. The Friendship West Baptist Church in Dallas Texas, led by Reverend Dr. Freddie Haynes III, has been one of the more outspoken proponents of rebuilding a Black Wall Street and encouraging and supporting black entrepreneurship. Dr. Haynes views himself as an extension of the prophetic preaching tradition of both Martin Luther King Jr and Malcolm X. Even the more moderate churches such as the Oak Cliff Bible Fellowship led by Tony Evans is noted for the many businesses in the Dallas Texas area that has grown out of its ministry. The Potter's House of Dallas Texas is a mega-church led by Bishop TD Jakes, which testifies to hundreds of black businesses within the congregation due to the encouragement, training ministry and teaching of Bishop Jakes.

Jakes has written books on this topic of economic empowerment, one of which is entitled *"Soar, How to Build your Vision from the Ground Up."* Malcolm X was also a product of prison education and a model for how former criminals can be reformed and reenter society as productive members of the community. Bishop Jakes has founded a non-profit organization where those who are in prison can educate themselves and be prepared for successful re-entry post prison. While the voices of Evans and Jakes are not as radical and militant as Haynes and Wright, their practical theology falls and line with the tradition of community empowerment through religious organizations.

Black Zionism and Reparations

The black Muslim movement also taught its followers that critical to black Independence, empowerment and self-reliance is the demand for reparations. The concept that was promoted by the black Muslims stated that rather than focusing upon assimilation by black people into white society, blacks should demand reparations in the form of its own mini nation state by granting them their own geographical territory within the United States as repayment for the harms that have been inflicted upon the black race due to slavery and as an answer to the historic hostility inflicted upon the black community as a legacy of slavery. Based on Cone's research, the Black Muslims, solution to the problem of black oppression in America, therefore, is territorial separation, either by whites financing black people's return to Africa or by providing separate states in America. Based on the mythology of the mad scientist Yacob, European descendants could not be reformed, and therefore separation was the only remedy.[113] A better theory might suggest that the European invention or pseudo-science of a racialized humanity, has made it nearly impossible to live harmoniously under one banner.

Black Zionism, as it is often called, has always had a history in America. The black Muslims' idea was a continuation of this geographical vision for black liberation.

They believed that if this independent status were to occur, they would never again be marginalized by a majority culture who did not embrace them as fully human, nor would they have to rely politically or economically upon those who exercise racial hostility or unjust control over their communities. This was not a radical idea as some may think. This concept was historically embraced by black clergy in conjunction with white missionaries, the US government and wealthy benefactors after the Civil War. The founding of the African nation of Liberia was a result of the theology of black Christians.

The AME Zion Church was one of the original advocates for this idea. Their view, along with that of white missionaries, was that black people should repatriate to Africa because of the predictable difficulties that would arise between the races post-emancipation. Bishop Henry Neal Turner, according to theologian Demetrius K.

---

[113] Cone, Martin, Malcolm and America, 28

Williams, advocated for Black Zionism by stating that emigration to

Africa was the only satisfactory solution to the race problem in America because there is no manhood future in the United States for the Negro. He may eke out an existence for generations to come, but he can never be a man, full, symmetrical and undwarfed. [114] Liberia was founded by freed black people in 1847, as states were beginning to ban the trafficking of their people. These freed persons began to immigrate to that area along the West African coastline as early as 1822.

Black Zionism, generations prior to the black Muslim demand, had forever existed in the imagination of African descendants in America. This Zionist vision, which lived in the hearts of black people, was expressed and supported by notable figures such as Fredrick Douglass. Because of the unjust way in which the courts of the United States related to black freedom, a separate land to which black people could emigrate elsewhere seemed logical. The 1857 Dred Scott Case, which was argued before the Supreme Court, clearly stated that black people would not be acknowledged as citizens in the United States nor entitled to any basic rights as humans. Professor Edward Onaci, a professor of African American history at Ursinus College, states the following regarding black Zionism and its direct relationship to the Dred Scott case and other similar rulings in the American court system:

---

[114] Williams, Demetrius. True to Our Native Land-A New Testament African American Commentary (Brian K. Blount, Ed.) Minn. MN: (Fortress Press, 2007), 241

While they could be citizens of individual states which determined their status and well-being, as noncitizens of the Union, black people had no rights which white men were bound to respect. In the aftermath of Dred Scott, black folks who before were skeptical of emigration began packing their bags and looking for homes in Liberia, Canada, and elsewhere. Even Frederick Douglass for a short time gave 'qualified support' to black people's emigration to Haiti. [115]

The paradox surrounding the founding of Liberia is that many of the black free persons who repatriated to that area brought with them the imperialistic influences from the United States of America, where many of the black free persons felt that they were superior to the native Africans and treated them accordingly. Most had not been educated out of their slave society mindset they had developed from American racism and self-defeating anti-African thought. This experience in Liberia's history with black American Freedmen, gives credence to Elijah Muhammad's view that before black Zionism can be achieved, there must first be a mental liberation from the "white man's" colonial world view, which must be replaced with a moral, spiritual and psychological awakening. The Harlem Renaissance, Garveyism, and the Black Muslims were the first to sound the trumpet for this awakening. The tension between the descendants of American freedmen and native Liberians eventually led to conflicts between the American freed persons and their

---

[115] Onaci, Edward. *Free the Land: The Republic of New Afrika and the Pursuit of a Black Nation State.* Chapel Hill, NC: (UNC Press Books, 2020), 79

descendants and the native Africans as late as the 1990s with the civil war which overthrew President Charles Taylor. This phenomenon led to a reverse emigration of "Americo-Liberians," whose population exists mostly in America today. The black Muslim program advocated for the re-education of black people before the establishment of a new nation upon the American continent. Perhaps this would have been in retrospect the model for repatriation during the 1820s prior to the foundation of Liberia. This idea has largely been abandoned by black churches of today, but the call for reparations which includes individual land for slavery descendants continues to this day.

The black Muslims advocate for this idea of black Zionism, which is a part of their "program," in their Final Call newspaper. It first appeared in Muhammad's book "Message to the Black Man in America":

Since we cannot get along with them in peace and equality, after giving them 400 years of our sweat and blood and receiving in return some of the worst treatment human beings have ever experienced, we believe our contributions to this land and the suffering forced upon us by white America, justifies our demand for complete separation in a state or territory of our own [116]

While many Christian bible teachers adhere strictly to the concept of establishing a spiritual kingdom on Earth, the divine ideal of inhabiting one's own land in a state of freedom is a persistent

---

[116] . *Elijah Muhammad, Message to the Black Man in America 1965.* *https://noi.org/muslim-program/*

theme throughout scripture. In fact, Abraham, the father of the world religions, established the principal of laying respectful land boundaries as the key to familyhood. When Abraham and Lot's herdsmen had strife among them concerning their land boundaries and cattle, he encouraged both sides not to allow any strife to exist between them, but to go in their own direction and his household would go in theirs, because we are family (Gen. 13:8.)

The conquest of others to solve the problem of landlessness or to extend the empire is inconsistent with the concept of love and reverence for humanity. Displacement of others is a crime against God and humanity However, all people have the right to develop their own nations, dwell in their own land and live in harmony with their human neighbors. Eurocentric eschatology has not only attempted to get black people to forget about the hell of slavery and dehumanization on earth in the prospect and hope of heaven, but it has also de-emphasized the importance of land for the oppressed and displaced. It is true that ideals of black Zionism are held among a minority of black people, yet the vision has always been alive in the black imagination. The founding of Liberia by black Christians, the tenets of black Muslims and black nationalist groups are examples of that history. Onaci has written extensively on the work of black nationalists seeking to establish a black nation within the borders of the United States called the Republic of New Afrika. Notice the heroines and heroes of the movement which are mentioned and the details of the vision by those who would identify as "New Afrikans:"

During the final weekend in March 1968, five hundred activists and Pan-African nationalists came together at the Black Government Convention to determine the destiny of the 'captive black nation' in America. Participants included Lawrence Guyot of the Student Nonviolent Coordinating Committee and director of the Mississippi Freedom Democratic Party, Betty Shabazz [wife of Malcolm X,] Maulena Karenga, Amiri Baraka, and highly revered reparations activist 'Queen Mother' Audley Moore...to discuss their historic political conditions and legal remedies available under international human rights law. After deliberating about religion, culture, sexism and government repression, on Sunday March 31, several dozen attendees in convention agreed to sign a document declaring to the world that they would struggle for the complete independence and statehood of the black nation, which they named the Republic of New Afrika...By calling themselves 'captive,' New Afrikans were indicating that they were members of an internal colony that like colonized nations elsewhere had the right to self-determination...The people who signed the Declaration of Independence believed they could create an independent black nation state from Louisiana, Mississippi, Alabama, Georgia, and South Carolina and that a significant portion of the African-descended population would join them...Equally important, they advocated for a reparations settlement for the United States role in the international trafficking of African peoples, their enslavement in the United States, and the persistent violence, degradation, socioeconomic inequality, an consistent efforts to suppress black self-determination.[117]

It must be noted that Queen Mother Audley Moore, a Christian leader in her own right, who was a friend of Rosa Parks, Jesse Jackson and Nelson Mandela, was also a founding member of the Republic of New Afrika. Amazingly, the founding members honored this revered Christian woman alongside the widow of Malcolm X, Betty Shabazz. Queen Moore saw her advocacy for the Republic of New Afrika as consistent with the biblical ideal of advocating on behalf of the poor and marginalized for the purpose of human rights and self-determination. Audley Moore was also a Garveyite and a member of the United Negro Improvement Association, which was predominantly Christian. Audley Moore was also a major participant in the Million Man March in 1994. We find in this history, black Christian Zionists and Garveyites influencing the Black Muslim movement, and the black Muslim movement reminded black Christians of their sacred roots in this work.

Queen Audley Moore, upon hearing the text of the founding document for New Afrika, could be heard shouting, as if in a church service, "Hallelujah, Hallelujah...I lived to see the day," and proceeded to be the first signatory to the document. *In fact, On March 29, 1969, New Afrikans assembled at New Bethel Baptist Church, Reverend C. L. Franklin's ecumenical home during a weekend- long celebration of the Republic of New Afrika's first*

---

[117] Onaci, 17

anniversary.[118] Each of the groups, Muslims, Christians, or secularists, which were represented in the founding of New Afrika, were either rooted in black religion or grew out of it.

Head of the Theology and Religious Studies Department at King's College in the UK, who is also a noted ethicist and sociologist-professor Linda Woodhead and R. Kendall Soulen, who is a professor of Systematic Theology at Emory University co-edited a project which highlights the sin of displacement and landlessness.

Their conclusions and ethics are in line with the visionary work of the "New Afrikans." Soulen and Woodhead's work noted the following:

[Hebrew prophet] Jeremiah's expressions of anguish and mourning at the separation of land and people attest to the depth of the bond between the two, as do his visons of Israel's restoration which always included a landed dimension...Jeremiah challenges our Christian assumption that issues of land and place are of little consequence for human life...To ignore or deny that human existence is grounded in the particular places that support our physical, social, and cultural existence is an abstraction of our human condition beyond recognition.[119]

Soulen and Woodhead's theological view lends support to the vision of a New Afrika for the descendants of the enslaved in America. African Americans or New Afrikans, according to history

---

[118] Ibid, 32
[119] Soulen, R. Kendall and Woodhead, Linda. *God and Human Dignity.* Grand Rapids MI: (Wm. B. Eerdmans. 2006), 137-138

have been historically deprived of both citizenship rights, restorative justice through reparations. Because of the systematic discrimination and imprisonment of Black people by the powerful, it is reasonable to consider a separate independent state where black people can formulate their own leaders, government and laws without the prospect of white backlash and white fear. It is hypocritical to say that it is unloving to formulate one's own government on their own land, when people groups all over the world have managed to do so while maintaining their Christian identity. Self-government is not unloving nor unchristian. Soulen and Woodhead agree that such self-government and land possession is fundamental to human existence which cannot be denied an any theological basis.

One footnote in Woodhead's volume states that *Liberation theologians of recent decades have begun to assert the importance of land for human life, because salvation includes not only a heavenly reward but also temporal dimensions including health, social and economic fairness and peace on earth.*[120]

If theologians support a theology of land for human life on behalf of refugees and asylum seekers, then certainly the same should apply to descendants of Africa who have suffered from violence under America's racism structures and its denial of human rights. Therefore, one can be undeniably Christian and simultaneously advocate for black self-rule as a means of repair and restitution. It

---

[120] Ibid, 138

has often occurred when black activists challenge America on its present-day racism, that prejudiced White's will say, "If you don't like it here, go back to Africa," or "Go live in another country where you can appreciate." White people protest and share their grievances all the time, but too many do not respect black people's right to do the same. They feel that they are the benefactors of black people and that they should be grateful to live in their land. Some have indeed left and made their homes in Africa during the "Year of Return" in 2019, (four-hundred years since the 1619 arrival of enslaved Africans in Jamestown VA) and thousands left between 2019 and 2020, not because of White people's challenge to leave, but to flee anti-black violence by the state. What so many fail to realize is that they do not have the right to demand anyone go anywhere, because America has a debt to pay to the children of the enslaved who have developed and built the country Additionally, the indigenous population holds the view that the land America occupies is stolen.

For many, this debt that the American government owes includes a significant land grant for the purpose of self-rule. Onaci mentions Quebec, Catalonia and South Sudan as modern examples of political self-determination within larger national and geographical contexts and that taken together, *issues of sovereignty, self- determination, national identity and attempts to maintain the global status quo through legal and extralegal enforcement demonstrate that the basic idea behind New African independence and self-determination, is more commonplace than some may realize.* [121]

This is consistent with the view of the Hebrew prophets who saw landlessness as an aberration to a value system which affirms human dignity and flourishing. Many Christians advance the idea that loving one another and inhabiting land together is the highest ideal, however one can pursue self-determination and embrace each other as neighbors at the same time. Canadians, Mexicans and Americans may love each other and yet pursue their own unique destinies as a distinct people in their own land.

When I see the President of the United States and a black VP having to sit down in the White House to negotiate the nation's budget with allies of domestic terrorists and nationalists, and a Speaker of the House who had to concede to them to obtain his position, which reminds me of how the North negotiated with the South at the expense of the newly freed, and when I see a black secretary of defense, of whom we are proud, has to lead an imperialistic war machine, and when I consider how our president Obama had to lead the charge against Quaddafi-an ally of Nelson Mandela, and how gentrification of Washington DC happened under Adrian Fenty and black leadership who rely on their money in order to lead municipalities, I wonder whether those who advocated for a separate anti-colonial, anti-greed, pro-freedom, pro-Afrikan and independent state, such as Fredrick Douglass, the early AME Zion leaders, Elijah Muhammad and Malcolm X had conceptualized a

---

[121] Onaci, 21

more rational option for Afrikan descendants, because the "burning house" metaphor seems more relevant today than ever, but I am reminded that the tide is turning and there is hope. Such present-day musings are not unusual among native or generational Black Americans.

Black Churches and Black Lives

Throughout the history of black resistance, what was once considered extreme or radical, eventually became normalized. This is especially true of the reparation idea, which has been considered by cities, state governments and American universities. Black Lives Matter was once considered radical following Trayvon Martin's killing, but now is a major part of the American political, sociological and religious culture. When the Black Lives Matter movement began after the vigilante lynching of Trayvon Martin, they were viewed as radical by the liberal and conservative political establishment.

However, there were already clergy who had been influenced by both Dr. King and Malcolm X who were preaching the same sentiments even before the Black Lives Matter movement began. However, the fact that they were in the streets, not feeling the burden to call for peace and calm as was often unfairly the case for black clergy. Black Lives Matter advocates seemed to sympathize with the anger expressed by black people in the streets. Not feeling the need to apologize for vandalism due to black rage [and in many cases manufactured by counter-protesters] of which they played no role, they continued to amplify and confront the murderous brutality by the state.

Unlike many black clergy in the past, Black Lives Matter organizations had no qualms in holding white supremacy accountable for the outrage and vandalism which occurred and laying it at their feet of advocates for police violence. They pointed out the inhumanity of the selective horror which whites expressed concerning property damage at protests rather than being horrified by young unarmed black people losing their lives to state violence. Black lives activist, Tamika Mallory, who grew up in Sharpton's National Action Network organization, gave an unforgettable speech that shook the nation. Her words, which went viral, resonated with so many who were frustrated that there was more concern shown for broken windows than black life itself. In the spirit of Malcolm X, Mallory passionately addressed the issue at a press conference in Minneapolis during the 2020 protests concerning the George Floyd killing:

We are not responsible for the mental illness that has been inflicted upon our people by the American government, institutions and those people who are in positions of power... Do what you say this country is supposed to be about — the land of the free for all. It has not been free for Black people, and we are tired. Don't talk to us about looting. Y'all are the looters. America has looted Black people. America looted the Native Americans when they first came here, so looting is what you do. We learned it from you. We learned violence from you. We learned violence from you. So, if you want us to do better, then, damn it, you do better. [122]

Although Mallory was close to 40 years old at the time, her youthful appearance, combined with her cornrows, gave the impression that she was speaking these words as a young teen when she said, "We learned it from you!" These militant voices, such as Mallory, provided amplification to the prophetic preaching and advocacy of black churches and their voters. For a short period, black lives protesters and the black church began to play the role of good cop, bad cop as the street organizations were viewed as severely disruptive in city councils and political rallies and not taking a strong stance against property damage during protests.

Soon white churches and organizations begin to realize that the black church did not view Black Lives Matter as radical as they did; some moderate white churches, taking note, embraced the slogan. In fact, many placed the words "black lives matter" on church marquees and on banners upon their church buildings. These phenomena did not occur during the time of the Black Power movement. Churches at that time were not involved in the Black Power movement and would not consider placing the words "We want Black Power" on their marquees or banners. However, since the rise of the Black Lives Matter movement, especially since 2020 and beyond, pastors of black churches could regularly be seen wearing t-shirts with the words "black lives matter" emblazoned on

---

[122] Mallory, Tamika, Speech at Press Conference about George Floyd Police Murder. Minneapolis, MN, May 29, 2020.

them, including writing books on the topic. The reason the white establishment viewed them as radical, they claimed, is because they expressed on their website their belief in Marxism and not supporting traditional family values. However, most would agree, that these reasons for not supporting Black Lives protests are only a part of the issue, and that it is mainly due to the familiar reticence white Christians have concerning civil rights advocacy of black people.

What the white establishment failed to recognize is that black people do not fear Marxism in the same way that whites do. In fact, in the history of Black protest in America, there have been those who claimed to support Marxism to poke their fingers in the eye of the White political establishment. What both white liberals and conservatives fail to consider is that Black people have never lived in a Marxist society, but they have indeed lived under racism, Jim Crow, mass incarceration, lynching, chain gangs and Black Codes. Black people have the fear of a new Jim Crow more than white people fear Marxism. As it relates to traditional family values, black people understand that poverty wages and the prison industrial complex as anti-black family. Black clergy viewed the white Christian establishments enthusiastic support of the police in the face of repeated killings by them did not reflect a high level of value for black families, particularly black mothers who saw their children dying in the streets. Many were more offended by the words "Black Lives Matter" more that they empathized with the tears of black mothers. Black families cannot thrive if their male sons are trapped in underfunded schools and become victims of the high school to prison pipeline.

While Marxism is the supreme boogeyman for the white Christian establishment, the rise of what many black people foresee as system of white backlash, creates a higher level of fear that their rights will be reversed and that their children will live in a world far worse than the imagined Marxism that the white Christian establishment fears.

Nothing created this fear among black people more than the white Christian Evangelical efforts for the election of Donald Trump in 2016. This was because of Trump's racist rhetoric and support he received by people such as former Klan leader and White nationalist-David Duke and neo-Nazi groups. They observed how Donald Trump prior to his rise to the presidency sought to politically force President Obama's hand to reveal his birth certificate.

Diminishing or shaming powerful black people, has historically been the way in which many white people historically asserted their supremacy over them. Black voters saw this as a repeat of the history where black people had to show their papers when they were in white spaces to prove that they were legitimate or had permission to exist there.

Black voters were further angered by Trump's attack on black athletes and celebrities who were protesting police brutality. Placing pressure on the National Football League to come down on black athletes who are using the voices as advocates for the black community, was shameful in their view. Black athletes would kneel during the national anthem, rather than stand and put their hands over their chest, which was done to highlight the problems of inhumane policing. Publicly attacking Colin Kaepernick as a show of strength to uber-patriotic whites, was a way Trump solidified his power among his followers. Diminishing popular black figures was a way of showing strength against a rising culture, and putting them in their place, became the standard for the right-wing political discourse.

Black clergy and voters also saw the Charlottesville Virginia protest called the "Unite the Right rally" where white nationalist groups were protesting the removal of confederate general Robert E Lee's statue. Nationalists and sympathizers of Confederate history believed that this was a scheme which would be the result of erasing the best of American history and a symbolic act that was a part of removing white people from power. Advocating for pro- Apartheid whites in South Africa who claimed they were victims in the post-Apartheid era, Trump threatened that he would intervene against black South African leadership. This was a bridge too far for Black clergy and voters. The fear of where this was heading frightened many black people and they understood that they needed the most militant response to such a prospect during the 2020 elections.

Donald Trump also claimed to be an advocate for what was his own imaginary and antiquated view of white female suburbanites, stating that he would keep lower income earners from moving into their neighborhoods. This was strangely familiar to black people who remember the history when black people were not allowed to move into white neighborhoods and would be confined to certain areas.

Promises of redlining was what Trump promoted during his 2020 election campaign. A champion for harsh police tactics, he fulfilled his promise to deal with protesters by sending federal marshals into areas to attack protesters where he believed mayors were being too soft. One example of this occurred in Washington DC during the Black Lives Matter protest where riot police with harmful chemical weapons moved violently against the protesters who were peaceful and nonviolent in Lafeyette Square (now Black Lives Matter Plaza.) Marxism was not now more fearful than the present reality. For these reasons, black clergy would embrace advocacy for Black Lives rather than join their white contemporaries in condemning the movement.

At this moment in 2020, the good cop and bad cop were one and the same. White protestants view Marxism as anti-Christian, while black clergy view racism, advocacy of a brutal police state and white supremacy as both anti-black and anti-Christian.

Black Muslims and Black Lives Matter

Although the large percentage of black Muslims today have embraced orthodox Islam, they do not receive support from among the broader Muslim community when injustices are committed against them due to their God-given blackness. This is similarly true when the white church is silent when injustices are committed against black people, which becomes one area where black Muslims and black Christians are on an island by themselves. It should not be lost on observers how white Christians raised $400,000.00 to support 19-year-old Kyle Rittenhouse, who fired an AR-15 and killed a black lives matter protester, and wounded another, also slandered the child of Sybrina Fulton--the Baptist Christian mother of slain 17-year-old Trayvon Martin. Such empathy was not on display when it came to this devoted Christian mother and her family; they identified with those who saw heroism in the rifle-wielding youth who they saw as standing up to the protesters. Traditionally speaking, evangelicals align with those who condemn black protest, and those who blame black people who are subject to state violence. Sadly, black Christians and black Muslims do not receive the support they should from within their larger faith communities.

Within this context, black Muslims made a statement in support of the movement for black lives. They highlighted and decried how non-blacks within the Muslim community remained silent when the community was suffering so much turmoil. Drawing the attention of the public to the issues with police violence, they laid out the history of brutality against black Muslims, namely the 1962 police murder of Ronald Stokes. This event is what sparked Malcolm X to visit Los Angeles and stand with the protesters, who were black Muslims and black Christians. Amadou Diallo, another black Muslim slain by police in 1999, was also mentioned by black Muslim Advocates. Calling for Police Reform and making a stand against state violence against black people, they made the following declaration concerning reform or abolish:

*We recognize that discrimination pervades our entire justice system — from policing to trials to prisons to re-entry barriers for returning citizens — and that these demands only represent a down payment on the reforms that are needed. If this deep-seated discrimination cannot be done away with through reform, then these systems will need to be abolished and reimagined entirely. As American Muslims, we will draw on our diversity, our strength, and our resilience to demand these reforms because **Black lives matter.**[123]*

What is incredibly significant about orthodox black Muslims making such a political statement expressing that Black Lives Matter is their own socially conscious origins. Most orthodox black American Muslims have their origins in Malcolm X's post-Mecca conversion and Wallace Muhammad, the successor of NOI founder, Elijah Muhammad. Today, the orthodox black Muslims and black Christians are aligned in their call for police reform or abolition.

Defund and Reform

Abolish or defund the police activists may well be the bad cop actor in the movement advocating for black lives, while the mainstream black political leaders and clergy may represent the good cop in this sociological interplay. While these slogans may be repugnant even to the black middle class, there are those who may

---

[123] *(Muslim Advocates Police Violence Statement, 2008)*

not necessarily condemn them due to the necessity of having the contrast. Nothing frightens the white evangelical voter class than this idea. The militant police state is viewed as their only security against the poor and black population; they cannot imagine their survival without it. In their imagination, they see hordes of black and poor people roaming their neighborhoods terrorizing, harassing, committing violence and robbing them of everything valuable from their homes.

While defund and "abolish the police" movements have studied and researched people-oriented community alternatives that will keep neighborhoods safe, most are so fearful of the language because they've never read or studied the topic. Additionally, the relationship between policing and plantation economics is clear. Hardware, technology, artillery, tanks and other military equipment connects policing to the pipelines of the military industrial complex.

Abolitionists argue that police rarely prevent crime and violence but only respond or create violence. Highway stops do not occur due to responses to violent crimes occurring on the roads, but due to the hunt for criminals, which is connected to predatory economics. Therefore, a taillight being out, the wrong speed combined with a wrong answer to the police can turn deadly, and black people are the primary targets. Consequently, due to the lack of being able to imagine a world without cops, and its consequential fears, politicians are more open to discussing other matters concerning police tactics and priorities. Therefore, clergy, street-level activists and black professionals are viewed somewhat as a saner alternative.

One can easily imagine that Malcolm X and the Black Panthers of old would have indeed advocated or in the very least expressed sympathy for the idea of abolishing the police. As he once stated, as a field slave, in contrast to the house slave, he would not be mad if the master's house burned down. If discussions of police and prison reform are not welcomed, there are others who are willing to change the subject to a more dramatic transformation.

Since 2021, filmmaker Bree Newsome Bass, has advocated for abolition. Bass initially gained visibility in the aftermath of the Mother Emmanuel A.M.E Church in Charleston SC, which was subject to a murderous racist rampage in 2015, when she climbed the flagpole at the South Carolina state capitol building and removed the Confederate Flag. As an activist and filmmaker, she has traveled as a public speaker on black and human rights. Some believed that her act of civil disobedience and direct action brought attention to the problem of the flag, which shortly thereafter led to its official removal. *Abolition for the People: The Movement for a Future Without Policing and Prisons,* a book authored by Colin Kaepernick, is part of the inspiration behind Newsome's abolition work.

According to Newsome and other abolitionists, the problem with the criminal justice system does not stem from a few bad apples, a lack of training, or the way resources are allocated. The idea is that the institution itself is owned and controlled by the ruling class which constitutes white politicians and corporate America, and thus the system will never change as long as the elite profit and that the damage is limited to black and poor people.

As abolitionists see it, politicians are controlled by the money which continues to expand and weaponize the system. Newsome observes that police executions on the street have increased since the George Floyd killing, and this is the greatest evidence that it is impossible to change policing in America. During the aftermath of the George Floyd killing, politicians from both sides of the aisle came together and agreed upon the need to reform. The outrage surrounding Floyd's death became a worldwide protest; people from different countries marched in the streets for reform. If this could not change the system, with all the subsequent engagement on the issue, nothing could. Newsome stated in one powerful tweet, *"The white owner class is not policed or surveilled because the function of police is to maintain the race/class hierarchy and protect only the property of the wealthy, not the property of the poor which they regularly damage."[124]*

The fact that such ideas had entered the American discourse frightened both liberals such as Bill Maher and conservative viewers of Fox News. Liberal politicians became so alarmed, that they began to blame black people for their election losses. It was quite inconvenient for them to have such a discussion on a topic raised by abolitionists during a crime wave. Even president Joe Biden, who rose to the White House on the backs of Black voters and the 2020 protesters, risked alienating them as he attempted to reassure the

---

[124] https://twitter.com/BreeNewsome/status/1618991962497097730

nervous and paranoid owner class that it was his plan to give more funding to policing rather than defund the police. While black clergy do not generally advocate for abolition, their ideas for police reform become more palatable and mainstream than the alternative. Black clergy, while not advocating to defund, do not generally agree, as Biden suggested, that more funding is productive. [125]

The cries for unconditional and unquestioning support of the police are a part of securing whiteness against everything else, and therefore to call for the abolishing of the police sounds too much like abolishing whiteness itself. Whiteness requires that the so-called violent black underclass and the rising black middle class be kept in their places, and the police are indispensable in this endeavor.

And there is the paradox that many of you refuse to see: to get to a point where race won't make a difference, we have to wrestle, first, with the difference that race makes. The idea that whiteness should be abolished, an idea that some white antiracist thinkers have put forth, disturbs a lot of you—especially when you argue that whiteness is not all murder and mayhem. [126]

What Dyson alleges is that what makes so many uncomfortable is the threat that should the pain of black people be understood, that whiteness, which has been the source of the pain, will be questioned. In some cases, the police are viewed as the guardians of whiteness,

---

[125] (https://www.whitehouse.gov/briefing-room/speeches-remarks/2023/02/07/remarks-of-president-joe-biden-state-of-the-union-address-as-prepared-for-delivery/)
[126] Dyson, 77

to the extent that to question police activity means that whiteness is not being given the appropriate respect.

Dyson Sociology and Whiteness

Dyson further explains how within American society, whiteness requires that black people diminish themselves to a certain degree to avoid being offensive. As Terry Melvin of the Coalition of Black Trade Unionist once said, *A paranoid minority wants us silenced everywhere except on a stage or basketball court.* Black people remaining in their places and not exercising their full humanity, has been the means of providing comfort and security for whiteness since America's inception.

The police presence in its present form is the guarantor of that security and superior position. Consequently, so many are appalled when a black motorist asks questions about why they are being pulled over or whether they are under arrest. Whiteness views such questions as disrespectful and out of place, and whatever consequence is inflicted, whiteness says that the black motorist deserves it for daring to declare their humanity and equal rights. The motorist must acknowledge the superior position of the police and his/her own inferior position within that space. Dyson describes such encounters with the following words:

We learn how to modify our speech in the face of cops. We temper our passion and modulate our tone so that we barely register as being there...We must believe that cops are gods; we are nothing. And the more we remember our nothingness, become experts in the philosophy of nothingness, the better chance we have to survive. [127]

Sometimes this learned behavior by blacks within white spaces is a subconscious survival mechanism passed down from prior generations. Malcolm was instrumental in liberating black people from this submissive posture, even though the residual effects of this learned behavior remain. Furthermore, Dyson explains that because Malcolm was unapologetically passionate about his love for black humanity, he was viewed as a hateful and violent figure by the white majority and by some blacks. Part of this love for black humanity, which was expressed by Malcolm, was designed to break the mental imprisonment of black people by leading them to love their own blackness and community.

This idea of black love espoused by Malcolm, was seen as a threat by many whites, as Dyson describes. Embracing the right to self-defense does not make one violent, yet Malcolm was viewed as such. Malcolm advocated for self-defense, but never engaged in violence as a public figure, and King who rejected strategic violence, retained his own personal armed security.

Remembering that Dr. King also believed in self-defense, while rejecting it as a strategy for black freedom, Dyson refers to Ossie Davis' speech at Malcolm's funeral:

As Ossie Davis said in his eulogy, responding to the claim that Malcolm preached hate and was a fanatic and a racist: "Did you even talk to Brother Malcolm? Was he ever himself associated with

---

[127] Dyson, 180

violence or any public disturbance?' The rage that flowed in Malcolm's veins was the rage against a force of whiteness that aimed to wash its black kin from the face of the earth."[128]

Both Malcolm and Martin were misunderstood; both men expressed rage and anger about the condition of black people in America. Dyson emphasizes that neither engaged in violence. The difference was tone, demeanor and rhetoric as they expressed their anger. Dyson's view of the two men was that even though their views on the strategies toward liberation were different, both were extremely critical of the predominant society, and extreme lovers of black people. Dyson advances the idea that tone is often overestimated, because regardless of language or tone, offense will be taken when such critique is given. He utilizes his own personal experience to illustrate this fact.

Returning to the college where he attended which also subjected him to a ban due to the racial problems he suffered, Dyson illustrates how little had changed in the three decades that he had been ostracized. The response to his speech from the audience is typical in cases where whiteness is challenged, and blackness too long diminished is fully expressed.

Back at my alma mater Carson-Newman after being banned for 31 years, and even though I felt the time warp, I also got cause for hope. When I preached in the chapel, I was certainly far more blunt and vocal in challenging whiteness than I had been when I went to

---

[128] Ibid, 96

school there. I preached about the black prophetic mission and its demand for social change. I riled up some conservative white students. Many got up and walked out.[129]

In the example given by Dyson, even after 31 years passed, the sensitivities to the prophetic language on behalf of black humanity, remains too much for whites to bear. This illustration is informative, because it explains why Malcolm was viewed as a threat even though he never engaged in violence, and why so many saw King as a threat in his later years. Although much has changed, it remains to be seen whether Whites can have any empathy for the more vocal and blunt witness on behalf of black liberation. King was not beloved, but Malcolm was even less beloved due to his bluntness in critiquing whiteness as an evil.

---

[129] Ibid, 77

11 Black Solidarity

While the good cop bad cop scenario played out dramatically between the Civil Rights Movement and a black power/black Muslim movement in the 1960s, there is little need for this modality today. The leading and loudest proponent of black rights among clergy over the past 20 years from a political perspective has been the Reverend Al Sharpton.

The leader of the black Muslim movement and heir of Elijah Muhammad's principles and organization is the Minister Louis Farrakhan. When listening to rhetoric of both Reverend Al Sharpton and the Honorable Louis Farrakhan, when it comes to the defense of Black America, there are militant themes with both figures. Both sound quite similar rhetorically in their advocacy. The difference is that the Reverend Al Sharpton engages the political system, while Louis Farrakhan and his followers do not. Farrakhan's followers still look to separation from the American system altogether as the solution to the denial of the human rights of black people. Al Sharpton, on the other hand functions from the tradition and perspective of black Christianity, which requires political participation as a matter of life and death. Sharpton is an offspring of both the black church tradition and the ideas of the Black Power movement.

However, there is one case where black Muslims and black

Christians were aligned for political ends and that was during the election of Barack Obama in 2008. For the first time on record black Muslims of the Nation of Islam branch encouraged their followers to go out and cast votes for Barack Obama for the presidency of the United States. Since that time the black Muslim movement has been disengaged in the political process. Many were disappointed when President Obama, once in office, would later advocate and support NATO's mission against Gaddafi, whom they greatly respected as a leader of African liberation. The black Muslim movement could not resist, historically speaking, participation in the election of the first black president of the United States of America. Farrakhan expressed pride in the potential Obama possessed with the most powerful office in the world for global human rights and peace. He proudly attributed much of Obama's success in winning the presidency to black Muslim political involvement. In fact, Louis Farrakhan refers to his own personal encounter with Obama prior to his rise and states that he has in his possession a photograph with himself and Obama. This was historic for the black Muslim movement, because since the time of Elijah Muhammad, they have advocated disengagement with the American political process, and instead imagined forming their own nation within a nation. Thus, we have the name "Nation of Islam."

This nation within a nation, as presently constituted, they believe, lays the foundation for the time when God himself will intervene and bring them into their own land within the North American continent, where they will become a prosperous independent nation based on Elijah Muhammad's principles of Islam. Because they understood the historic nature of Obama's presidency and its legacy stemming from the Civil Rights Movement, which occurred during Farrakhan's youth, was too powerful a force to overcome. The NOI understood the historical significance in the same light that black Christians, and turned out in record numbers for the election.

Not only is Al Sharpton the most visible religious voice advocating for black human rights, but so is attorney Benjamin Crump, who is also based in the Black American Church. Sojourners publication, which commonly addresses black religious and political issues, says *Faith is more than a thread through Crump's life: It is his life's scaffolding. Crump grew up in the Pentecostal church and said that throughout his life, his grandmother "held onto the unchanging Word of God." To this day, Crump considers her the wisest person he has ever met, and the effect her faith had on him and his own belief is evident. The motto of Parks and Crump, the law firm he and his friend Daryl Parks founded and amicably ended more than 20 years later, was: "We help David fight Goliath and win."* [130] He is the most visible voice in the legal field and is considered the "Attorney General" for Black America. The rhetoric of Benjamin Crump is very similar to that Malcolm X. Crump has with magical adeptness, been able to combine the rhetoric of both Malcolm and Martin to advance the cause of black liberation.

Standing on the shoulders of black heroines and heroes, black

---

[130] https://sojo.net/magazine/february-2019/advocate-benjamin-crump-faith-christian

clergy, scholars and theologians feel free to express themselves in more militant ways. This is because of their history of trailblazers, and consequently they have more political and economic power than in the past. Black prophets are free to express themselves both in the language of Dr. King and Malcolm X, depending on the time and place. Malcolm and Martin were not far apart as many suggest and believe, therefore black advocates for human rights are able to creatively blend the tone of both figures. C. Eric Lincoln describes this blend as self-determination combined with self-affirmation; he goes on to describe how this combination will impact the future of the black church.

As one of the few totally black controlled and independent institutions, black churches played a major role in resistance. Politically, resistance has included both self-determination and self-affirmation. Since the Civil Rights Movement and the attempts to desegregate American society, the accommodative pressures on black people and black institutions have grown considerably. One of the major roles of black churches in the future will be as historic reservoirs of Black Culture and as examples of resistance and independence. [131]

James Cone understands that black Christianity in America has historically held within its belief system, that to experience the freedom that Jesus envisioned, there must be dialogue with others who are part of the same struggle. As Cone sees it, the gospel is all

---

[131] Lincoln, Black Church, 15

about freedom, and when other traditions affirm this truth, they are affirming the gospel.

I believe that Jesus Christ is at the heart of the black experience in North America. I believe that it was Jesus who gave slave preachers the power to proclaim freedom as the essence of the Gospel. Henry Clay Bruce recalls a black preacher saying, 'free from death,' 'free from hell,' 'free from work,' 'free from white folks,' 'free from everything.' [132]

While black Christians and blacks of other traditions agree on the area of freedom, Cone corrects the misrepresentations by freedom fighters outside of the church. He addresses the wrongly held views by non-Christian blacks that the black Church has historically embraced what they refer to as "the white man's religion." Black people's reinterpretation of Jesus within their own struggle is often ignored by black people outside of the Christian tradition. Cone contends that they too often overlook the distinction between the gospel of the enslaved and that of the slaveholder. Arguing that this misunderstanding is what weakens the freedom struggle rather than black Christianity itself, because it creates more division than unity, Cone states the following:

Christians must not beat nationalists over the head with Jesus and neither should nationalists turn their noses up at black Christians. It matters little to White oppressors whether we are nationalists or Christians ...Malcolm's message is still true today.

---

[132] Cone, God of the Oppressed, 314

The crucial point is that we are black, and that fact alone ought to keep us open to each other, not for the purpose of conversion, but for shared participation in finding out the best means of struggle. This openness is the crux of our authentic recognition of each other as brothers and sisters. [133]

Black unity is a Christian principle, therefore, according to Cone, the differences within the community should not be more important than the purpose of freedom. Although Malcolm X had moments in his speeches where he would criticize black Christian leaders for embracing what he viewed as a white man's religion, when the rubber met the road, he acknowledged the desperate need for black unity.

Malcolm's speech in Los Angeles in 1962, trumpeted the idea that the suffering black people experience is not because of religion, but a racist disregard for their sacred humanity. Malcolm famously said the following:

We're not brutalized because we're Baptist. We're not brutalized because we are Methodist. We're not brutalized because we are Muslims. We're not brutalized because we're Catholics. We are brutalized because we are black people in America. [134]

Malcolm speech in Los Angeles highlighted the enormous difference between our existence and our belief systems. One is fundamental to how we view God, but the other is fundamental to our actual existence as image bearers of the divine. That we cannot

---

[133] Ibid, 314
[134] Malcolm X, 1962

express our beliefs nor contribute to religion if we are sick, dying or suffer annihilation, was the view of King. Black unity is a safeguard to that existence in a world in which it is threatened. You must exist in order to express belief and live it out. For this reason, Dr. King stated in his Drum Major Instinct sermon, that if America continued in its violent path, *I'm sorely afraid that we won't be here to talk about Jesus Christ and about God and about brotherhood too many more years.*[135] Our humanity must be respected and preserved to worship its creator in any shape or form. When Dr. King met with the late great boxer, Muhammad Ali, who was an early disciple of Malcolm, whom King supported in his protest of the Vietnam War, he stated that we are from different religions, yet we are brothers advocating for the same freedom. Dr. King, Malcolm, the Muslim movement and black socially conscious groups were deeply engaged in protesting American imperialistic and capitalistic wars, particularly against those revolutionary groups in the world who were striving to be free from their colonial masters. One Saturday night while Ture was in the office in Atlanta, he received a late phone call from Dr. King. King started the conversation by saying: *"young man, what are you doing in the office so late?"* *"The people's work (Carmichael responded,) I'm working for the people."* *"Well, as it happens, so am I."* *(said Dr. King.)*

"Reverend, I'm surprised, shouldn't you be doing the Lord's

---

[135] Martin Luther King Jr., 1968

work?" "A distinction without a difference, Stokely." said King. [136]

Dr. King went on to invite Ture and members of the SNCC organization to the Ebenezer Baptist Church the following Sunday morning to stand with him in support of his anti- imperialism sermon about the oppressive Vietnam War. There in that church, on that morning, we find the visual link between the black church and the black power militants, as Ture and others attended in solidarity. The spirit of Malcolm X and the spirit of the black church's ancestry was together in one sanctuary resisting the powers of enslavement. It was extremely important for Dr. King to have the militant presence there in the church that morning to garner support on the street level and to amplify voices like Ture's which had been promoting similar ideas in preceding years. What is also revealing and evident in the conversation that Saturday night was that King believed that black militant figures and black power advocates were "doing the Lord's work" of liberation along with the black preachers in the movement. According to King, "working for the people" and "doing the Lord's work" were one and the same. This anti-imperialist emphasis had the effect of blurring the lines between the good cop/bad cop dynamic, as King became public enemy number one after his position on Vietnam and American imperialism. Like Malcolm, he connected racism at home with African colonization and imperialism abroad.

Both Black consciousness and black Christianity has its history

---

[136] Ture, 515

of alignment with God in their love for a people who were taught to hate themselves. Since God is love, then black love has its origin in God, and both movements are synchronized to this end. Dr. King often referred to himself as an "extremist" for not only the concept of universal love, but also for black people. Malcolm's speeches and autobiography showcase Jesus' extreme love for black people. Both Malcolm and Martin are a reflection, with different language and background, of this black love which lays down one's life for one's friends. This symbiosis between the two streams (same river) of black thought was not only necessary but was indispensable to the salvation and thriving of black life in America. A love that hated everything that diminished black dignity and black life that was represented by both, was much bigger than tactical disagreements that would otherwise divide. Moreover, such love is as much needed today as it has been historically. This love which is expressed within the Nation of Islam through extreme black solidarity, the entire community would do well be to imitate and implement. This would apply both within the church and among others who are yearning for black liberation. If solidarity in Europe brought down the Iron curtain of a freedom denying U.S.S.R, then black solidarity, which lives out Jesus' vision of sticking closer than sisters and brothers, can bring down the American prison and police industrial complex, housing discrimination and economic exploitation.

Beginning in the early 1950s, Malcolm X showcased his extreme love and reverence for blackness in his speeches which served to bring healing to those who were suffering from the disease of black inferiority and trauma. He described black skin as golden, rebuked black people for their own self-hatred, and persistently highlighted the richness of African heritage. By loving themselves individually, Malcolm believed that this would lead to loving each other collectively in solidarity. Malcolm stated that the time will come black people will awaken psychologically and truly learn to think independently as other races and nations have independent judgment. When this awakening occurs, according to Malcolm, the black man will identify and think as a black man and feel for other black people, which will cause them to embrace solidarity. Malcolm then makes the case that *"At that point you'll have a situation where if you attack one Black man, you are attacking all Black men."* All black men (in a gender-neutral sense) in Malcolm's analysis would include Muslims, churchgoers, secularists, rich, middle class, poor, southerners or northerners.[137] This concept as expressed by Malcolm, which tied love and pride of race to black solidarity, was emphasized by Dr. King during the last years prior to his assassination.

As Malcolm's interview addressed the need to re-center blackness and de-center whiteness to achieve freedom, Dr. King would also embrace this vision in some of his later speeches. Many would argue that this awakening to racial pride and solidarity revived during the Black Lives Matter protests after the police and vigilante killings of George Floyd, Breonna Taylor, and Ahmad

---

[137] (Malcolm X interview on October 11, 1963, by sociology graduate student Herman Blake and Professor John Leggett.)

Arbery. The mood during those 2020 protests was indeed that of solidarity with the feeling that these were attacks upon all black people. Red, black and green Garveyite flags were frequently flown during the protests as a symbol of racial pride and unity. Dr. King agreed with Malcolm X that this spirit of independent judgment and pride of race could not be achieved through local, state or national laws, but through self- discovery among black people throughout the country. King equated this spiritual awakening to the black people's true declaration of independence. There must be a widespread rejection of the lies that have been said about blackness to reassert black dignity and humanity and reclaim their rightful place under the sun. It must be fully believed, as King saw it, that black people have a great history of which to be proud, and that they should reassert themselves by rejecting the historical lies about Africa told by white society. Notice King's words to this effect:

No document can do this for us. No Lincolnian emancipation proclamation can do this for us. No Kennedisonian or Johnsonian civil rights bill can do this for us. If the negro is to be free, he must move down into the inner resources of his own soul and sign with a pen and ink of self-assertive manhood his own emancipation proclamation. Don't let anybody take your manhood. Be proud of our heritage. As somebody said earlier tonight, we don't have anything to be ashamed of. Somebody told a lie one day. They couched it in language. They made everything black, ugly and evil. Look in your dictionary and see the synonyms of the word black. It's always something degrading, low and sinister. Look at the word white. It's always something pure, high, clean. Well, I want to get the language right tonight. I want to get the language so right that everybody here will cry out, "YES! I'M BLACK. I'M PROUD OF IT. I'M BLACK AND BEAUTIFUL![138]

This concept of affirming the beauty of blackness is a theological concept found in the statement "I praise you because [my blackness] is fearfully and wonderfully made; your works [in creating such beautiful blackness] are wonderful, I know that full well (Ps. 139:14, NIV.)" (Brackets supplied with author's application.) King goes further to state that such a revelation is necessary to break the chains of the black inferiority programming that has been infused from outside the culture. Such a revelation is indispensable for black people to function fully in their God-given purpose and freedom. It is not enough to be free from the limitations of Jim Crow segregation, poverty and second-class citizenship, but one must also break free from the mental limitations of the stigma society has placed upon blackness. This is what Dr. King described as being "truly free." It is the very message that Malcolm had preached early in the streets of Harlem, and undoubtedly resonated with Martin. In King's view, if black people do not believe in their own "somebodiness," they will never rise to their full potential as God's children and as members of the human family. There must be both civic/social freedoms, and an inner freedom of the soul. This inner freedom, which King envisioned, comes through a connection with

---

[138] *(Dr. Martin Luther King Jr. speech, April 3, 1968, Memphis TN.)*

the noble history of Africa and its descendants. One cannot exist without the other. Notice King's words which he gave a year before his assassination. It was a call for every black person in America to "rise up" and resist the popular culture's negative stigma concerning blackness and reclaim their God given heritage and dignity. In another speech, King added the following:

We must never be ashamed of our heritage. We must not be ashamed of the color of our skin. Black is as beautiful as any color and we must believe it...And so every black person in this country must rise up and say I'm somebody; I have a rich proud and noble history, however painful and exploited it has been. I am black, but I am black and beautiful. [139]

Malcolm's prediction about the black awakening in the October 1963 interview appeared to be realized after his death with the rise of black consciousness. Black solidarity, which was born out of black pride, was on full display in some of King's post-Malcolm marches as well as his rhetoric. This solidarity between the traditional and more militant wings of the movement became a part of black history. Sadly, Martin Luther King Jr and Malcolm X did not get the chance to march together since Dr. King had been jailed when Malcolm came to the South to help with a voting rights campaign. He was assassinated several weeks later.

Stokely Carmichael, upon the death of Malcolm, became a disciple of his speeches and philosophy, along with his SNCC

---

[139] *(Martin Luther King Jr. Speech at Glenville High School on April 26, 1967.)*

companions. In fact, prior to his work with SNCC, Ture attended gatherings of black consciousness street preachers during his time in Harlem, during the time when Malcolm was building the NOI's Temple #7. On one occasion, he attended an event where Malcolm debated about strategies for liberation. Malcolm stated, "Before you were American, you were black...Before you were Republican, you were black. Before you were Democrat, you were black...[and as it related to strategy and solidarity,] Malcolm went on to state the following in the hearing of Ture and his companions:

My stand is really the same as that of twenty-two million so-called Negroes. It is not a stand for integration. The stand is that our people want complete freedom, justice and equality. That is, respect and recognition as human beings. That is the objective of every black person in this country. Some think integration will bring it about. There are others who think separation will bring it about. So integration is not the objective nor is separation the objective. The objective is complete respect as human beings.[140]

Ture absorbed and remembered Malcolm's words, which would later help him place integration in its proper context against those who made it the end objective. Before his connection to Dr. King, Ture maintained respect for Malcolm and similar street preachers. Ture managed to merge the militancy of Malcolm and the direct-action focus of Dr. King. King marching with Carmichael was the political equivalent to marching with Malcolm.

---

[140] Ture, 260

Although Dr. King did not find the slogan Black Power useful, since it was not easily defined, and required too much explanation for those who would misinterpret and impose their own definitions, he believed in the ideas behind them. *He never repudiated black power. Never. Despite pressure, given from his own staff, he never yielded to the hysteria,* the NAACP's public criticism, and the knee-jerk reactions to the media's fabrications, Carmichael reflected.[141] (Ture 513.) Carmichael would later acknowledge in his autobiography that "Dr. King's judgement about the *'unfortunate choice of language' proved to be prescient and, if anything understated."* [142]

Such misunderstanding of Martin's critique of Malcolm has also been exposed in May of 2022, according to an article in "The Guardian" by Gloria Oladipo. It has been recently discovered that Martin Luther King Jr's alleged statement about Malcolm had been embellished by the 1965 interviewer in Playboy Magazine-Alex Haley. Jonathan Eig, who researched the original manuscript of the interview in the archives at Duke University, found that in referring to Malcolm, King never described his rhetoric as "fiery, demagogic oratory." This misquotation or falsification has been utilized for decades as evidence that there was a stark division and animosity between the two freedom fighters or that King was a harsh critic of Malcolm. Moreover, Eig found that King never stated in the interview that Malcolm had done "a great disservice" to black

---

[141] Ibid, 513
[142] Ibid, 523

America, as falsely reported in history, in calling for them to "arm themselves." It was discovered that King complemented Malcolm as an articulate spokesman for black America, with the suggestion that he speak more about positive and creative solutions to the issues.

In other words, he encouraged Malcolm not to miss the opportunity to become more politically engaged, as he eventually became. Additionally, in deference to Malcolm, King stated in the interview that he does not presume to have all the solutions, and that he was open-minded about any knowledge Malcolm might offer. Eig concluded that this was the work of embellishing King's words and that it amounted to *"journalistic malpractice."*[143]

The same has been historically true of the portrayal of King's view of black power. Kwame Ture (Stokely Carmichael,) who popularized the slogan, continued to be an open ally and embraced by King despite his concerns surrounding it.

Carmichael, who later went by the name Kwame Ture, corrects the record on the misrepresentation of his relationship to Dr. King and King's relationship with black power advocates in his autobiography, and refers to King's close identification with their work and philosophy. King, according to Ture, was his chief mentor. On one occasion, after visiting the Ebenezer Baptist Church and hearing King preach, Carmichael recalled his conversation afterwards that helped him understand Dr. King better. King noticed

---

[143] *(Gloria Oladipo, The Guardian, May 10, 2023, Martin Luther King's famous criticism of Malcolm X 'just not true', author finds)*

that Carmichael had an inquisitive yet frustrated look on his face and asked him what he was concerned about. Carmichael replied:

"Well, Dr. King, I was in Ebenezer this morning...I didn't see one white face in the congregation...you head a religious institution and a social organization, all black.

Why, you are the epitome of Black Power...yet the press, they love you while they whuppin' my poor nappy head flat. Can you explain that? He cracked up, 'Well, Stokely, its simple. Maybe I just don't talk about it.'" [144]

Ture went on to explain that Dr. King disagreed with the slogan, but only for practical and tactical reasons It must be remembered that King was a shrewd tactician. King observed, along with Andrew Young, that most groups who actually have power usually don't talk about it, and in many cases will even deny it. Andrew Young confirms, in Ture's account, that King did not disagree with black power, but the need to voice it in those terms, because it is always counterproductive in a pluralistic society. While King, did not see value in the slogan for black power, he loudly and boldly proclaimed that "black is beautiful" and *"I'm black and I'm proud."* Such phrases, King undoubtedly believed, were not as open to misinterpretation as "black power.

Carmichael's militancy was not a deal breaker for King but was a key part of their connection with each other. King believed in the virtues of black solidarity beyond strategic difference. In fact, in

---

[144] Ture, 514

King's speech at the March on Washington in 1963, he referred to the black radicals as the "marvelous new militancy." Undoubtedly, this "marvelous new militancy," was a direct reference to the work of Malcolm X in the urban centers of America. Although King did not endorse the emphasis on self-defense and retaliation, he later stated that he understood that "riots were the language of the voiceless." Many wanted him to condemn riots, but he refused to do so, because too many refused to condemn the conditions that caused them. King wanted the American public to understand that the key to peace was justice, and the alternative was societal breakdown. Three weeks before he was assassinated, he stated the following words which is worthy to be quoted at length for the benefit of the reader:

"But it is not enough for me to stand before you tonight and condemn riots. It would be morally irresponsible for me to do that without, at the same time, condemning the contingent, intolerable conditions that exist in our society. These conditions are the things that cause individuals to feel that they have no other alternative than to engage in violent rebellions to get attention. And I must say tonight that a riot is the language of the unheard. And what is it America has failed to hear? It has failed to hear that the plight of the negro poor has worsened over the last twelve or fifteen years. It has failed to hear that the promises of freedom and justice have not been met. And it has failed to hear that large segments of white society are more concerned about tranquility and the status quo

than about justice and humanity.[145]

This sociological diagnosis by King, of the conditions that bring about riots are strikingly similar to that of Malcolm X. Neither of them called for violent riots but predicted that they would always be the inevitable result of violent oppression.

Amazingly, the Boston Tea Party, which was the first American riot, is celebrated as one of the greatest days in American history. King's words about "white society" being more concerned with peace and maintaining their own status, than love for the sacred humanity and lives of their black family, are as true today as in 1968. Black people are disillusioned when so-called white allies are not as angry as they are about injustices committed against them, particularly when they push back against black anger. Dismissiveness, backlash or indifference remains a normalized posture whenever black people seek to make their voices heard concerning their plight, regardless of tone or level of activism.

---

[145] King, Martin Luther, March 14, 1968, Grosse Point High School Gymnasium, Grosse Point Human Relations Council, Grosse Pointe MI.

12 Concluding Thoughts on Black Religion

In conclusion, we must ask ourselves the question, why do we need the interplay of good cop, bad cop anyway? Why did Dr. King have to walk through the minefield by which he had to be considerate of white fear, while simultaneously advocating for black people's humanity? In a country which professes religion and faith in God, it should not require a threat of more militant alternatives in order to live freely as his image bearers. It is inhumane to be disagreeable and foolish to be surprised about the anger that is expressed when one's humanity is violated, and such anger ought to be understood and respected by all groups. Malcolm was famous for being a mouthpiece for black trauma and anger, and the same was true of Dr. King after the 1963 March on Washington. Historian, scholar, and founder of "black power studies," Peniel E. Joseph of University of Texas at Austin, described the symbiosis of the two iconic figures when he said that *"Malcolm X and Martin Luther King Jr represented dual sides of the same revolutionary coin and should not be viewed as warring ideological souls."[146]* In fact, like Malcolm, King had a pan- African and anti-colonialist perspective

---

[146] Peniel, Joseph E. *The Sword and the Shield.* New York: (Basic Books, 2020), 9

that black freedom in America, is tied to African freedom abroad. In 1957, according to records at Stanford University's King Institute, he was invited by African freedom fighter and Prime Minister Kwame Nkrumah, to attend the inauguration of Ghana's independence. While there, he said to Vice President Richard Nixon, who was also in attendance, *"I want you to come visit us down in Alabama where we are seeking the same kind of freedom the Gold Coast is celebrating."*[147] Professor Joseph continued to explain in his thesis how after the death of Malcolm, Dr. King picked up the mantle and became the most provocative figure and most vigorous opponent of White supremacy, at home and abroad and began to view America through the same lens—that of a burning house of immorality, greed and racism.

Highlighting the fact that both men were strident opponents of police brutality, Peniel Joseph compares King's criticism of the southern sheriff's terrorism and Malcolm's critique of New York and Los Angeles police department's brutality against black Muslims as being synonymous and harmonious. Additionally, the Black Lives Matter marches of 2020, because of the heinous police killing of George Floyd in Minneapolis, stood on the "political shoulders" of Martin and Malcolm. Marches which numbered in the tens of millions were the largest mobilization of social justice protests in American history, according to Professor Joseph's analysis. That only through the power and presence of a liberating

---

[147] https://kinginstitute.stanford.edu/encyclopedia/king-attends-ghanas-independence-ceremony

Lord and savior Jesus Christ, could such a miracle on behalf of the brutalized occur, would be the view of many black theologians. These marches were not only a protest concerning the killing of Floyd in Minneapolis, but the unleashing of a powder keg that had been building for many years of videoed killings of unarmed black people. If Martin or Malcolm were alive today, Joseph declares that they would have marched with the tens of millions who joined the Black Lives Matter protestors. Those among the Evangelical political base who declare that the protests on behalf of black lives goes against King's vision for a color-blind society, do not understand nor appreciate his work. King was not color blind in his "I Have a Dream" speech when he began by condemning police brutality against black people, nor when he stated emphatically that "black is beautiful." He did not attack the recognition of color barriers, but called out the sins perpetuated by those American color lines which kept black people from liberation. King was indeed color conscious, and cried out against a system which brutalized people because they were black. As Peniel Joseph sees it, many fail to realize that Malcolm was just as engaged in the movement for voting rights as was Martin, and Martin cried out against the criminal justice system as much as Malcolm. Once Malcolm was assassinated, the good cop persona ended for Dr. King, as he realized the degree to which racism had been entrenched in America. In fact, Joseph argues a point that describes this symbiosis that existed:

"Martin Luther King Jr.'s radicalization, in part due to his

relationship with Malcolm X, remains one of the most misunderstood aspects of King's legacy...Malcolm, the boldest critic of white supremacy in postwar America, helped inspire and ratchet up King's revolutionary politics. "[148]

Both men were unwavering critics who held rallies and marches against police brutality, and unwaveringly condemned the "white power structure" that targeted black people through law enforcement. Fatefully, the two would be targeted by the top law enforcement agency in America—the FBI, because they were viewed as threats to the social order. FBI director, J. Edgar Hoover, feared the rise of a "black messiah" in the same way that the biblical Pharaoh of Moses' day and Herod of Jesus' day feared such a figure who would destroy the social order and liberate the enslaved, exploited and dehumanized. The words of these icons were perceived as being as much a threat as their actions.

The predominant society, (especially those who claim to belong to Jesus) rather than recoiling from hearing about its problematic history and social ills, should respectfully listen to those who are a voice for the suffering ones, regardless of tone. The first step to healing is an honest diagnosis. Without the varied tonal expressions of resistance, the larger society would never receive the full measure of the lived realities of its fellow black citizens. Political politeness has its place, but should never be the school that African descended people are required to attend in order to graduate into a world where

---

[148] Joseph, 12

their lives are equally valued. Jeremiah and Amos were among the Hebrew prophets who struggled to moderate their own anger as they preached against the oppression of the poor. The good cop/bad cop sociological framework was useful for the mid-fifties and early sixties, but the ground had shifted after the killing of Malcolm and the rise of American imperialism. Consequently, Dr. King was forced to shift with the times. In this shifting reality, Peniel Joseph further describes the "radical" King's work:

The radical King spoke truth to power to sitting American presidents, questioned the fundamental unfairness of capitalism, blasted the Vietnam War and lambasted militarism, racism, and materialism. King marched alongside Black Power activist Stokely Carmichael (later Kwame Ture) in the withering heat of Mississippi, accused the US Congress of being unapologetically racist, and planned a campaign of massive civil disobedience in Washington, DC, under the banner of poor people across racial spectrum. [149]

Just as King began to become more of a voice for the voiceless on the grass roots level and in the urban centers due to Malcolm's radical energy, Malcolm, due to King's influence, went beyond his work of prosecuting white America and decided to engage the political arena surrounding voting rights for black people.

Profoundly, Peniel Joseph describes the two men as *the most important political figures in America's second reconstruction (from the 1954 Brown decision to Kings assassination) who found*

---

[149] https://kinginstitute.stanford.edu/encyclopedia/king-attends-ghanas-independence-ceremony

deep kinship on the sacred ground of human rights, dignity and citizenship.[150] One might add that these two represent in a larger way, the byproducts and interlocking relational aspect of the black consciousness from the Harlem Renaissance and the slave religion of resistance in the South.

Advocating for black liberation should not always require political genius or adaptation, as human survival is at the forefront of the issue. The predominant society would benefit from actively listening to both the diplomatic and undiplomatic voices, because no one should have to monitor their tone when they are advocating for human rights. Even the so called "good cop" gets tired of playing the conciliatory role when facing a viciously inhumane, persistently ruthless and violent criminal. This "tiring" or political exhaustion at the level of resistance to justice is what Dr. King experienced, and what Fannie Lou Hamer described as being "sick and tired of being sick and tired." Human Rights for the desperate and dying are more important than avoiding the perception of insults. No group of human beings should be required to take a polite posture while they are hurting and dying; both Malcolm and Martin understood this. On one occasion Dr. King in a moment of righteous anger said, *"I'm tired of marching for something that should have been mine at birth."* Both the Hebrew bible as well as the gospels refer to those who were angry, not because of a loss of status or privilege, but for the righteous cause of liberation. Moses was righteously and

---

[150] Joseph, 14

justifiably angry with Pharaoh when he refused let the children of Israel, at the divine command, be loosed from their chains and allowed to go that they may worship Yaweh (Exodus 11:8.) King David, being oblivious to the fact that he was the object of Nathan's parable as the man who killed Uriah and stole his wife, became angry at the proverbial rich man who stole the only sheep that the poor man possessed (2 Sam. 12:31.) Jesus was angry with the temple currency exchangers when he cleansed the temple (John 2:13-22,) as well as the hypocrisy of the religious leaders of the day (Matt. 23.) This was not only an expression of his own anger, but the hidden anger of those who were being exploited. Paul became angry with his fellow apostle- Peter, who displayed cultural arrogance against the Gentile believers by separating himself from those he viewed as beneath him when other Jews showed up (Galatians 2). The anger of Moses, David, Jesus and Paul toward exploiters and exploitation is the same that Malcolm, and later Dr. King, displayed on behalf of black people. The rights to which black people are owed should not be denied them regardless of strategy or angry tone, because they are God given. We do not earn our rights as God's image-bearers because we creatively hide our anger and "say it nicely" in some parent-child cultural dynamic. Human rights being denied to God's image bearers should justifiably anger both those who are suffering and those who claim to love them.

Many in the predominant society behave as if human rights are in their power to grant if they so choose, yet theological anthropology tells us that they cannot be granted by fellow humans, but only suppressed. Black solidarity is needed, only because there are few allies or accomplices in the mission for black liberation. This solidarity is joined in collective anger, empathy, hope and a sense of black dignity.

The black church exists because a white church historically dehumanized black Christians, and today too many will not learn from them. The black Muslims existed because of the loss of African historical and religious identity due to enslavement and the consequent efforts by the exploited to recover what they perceived to be lost. Both the black church and the black Muslims are examples of the need for black group solidarity in order to survive together in a hostile world and to connect with those who sympathize most closely with their plight. The symbiosis between the two streams of thought might be reflected in the words of Dr. Martin Luther King's immediate successor in the SCLC, Rev. Ralph Abernathy, who after Muhammad Ali's victory over Joe Frazier when he awarded him a medal and called him a *'living example of soul power, the March on Washington in two fists."* Corretta Scott King gave an additional complement to this black Muslim fighter, who had been wrongfully deprived of his World Champion status, due to his resistance to being drafted into America's imperialistic campaign in Vietnam. She recognized him as victorious both in athletics and freedom's cause when she referred to Ali as *"a champion of justice and peace."*[151]

---

[151] Arkush, Michael. The Fight of the Century. Hoboken, NJ: (John Wiley and Sons, 2008), 59

Due to the dehumanizing realities experienced by African descendants in America, there is the felt need to stick together to survive or accomplish anything meaningful on behalf of the people. Additionally, there are so many who are either silent or stand in the way. Throughout the history of African descendants in America, there has always been the need for subtlety, cleverness and subterfuge in order to survive or move toward freedom. The enslaved understood how to smile or laugh despite their inner rage, to avoid the enslaver's guilt and subsequent anger. This existed on the slave labor camps called plantations and all through the history of working and moving in the white world. Such maneuvering should not be necessary for those who are simply seeking to live out their human existence to the fullness which the Creator intended.

All voices and approaches to black liberation are educational in nature for those who are willing to listen. Even when the impulse of offense arises, call upon the scriptural mandate, to allow every person to be apt to listen, slow to speak and slow to be offended. Black Lives Matter is a slogan that is offensive to those who deceive themselves into believing that America is a land of freedom for all but are not offended by the conditions which require that black life must be affirmed in this way. In a world where black life is valued and black love can flourish, the sociological reality of good cop/bad cop scenarios as the title of this volume suggests, would not exist. More importantly, we refuse to suffer in silence, to cater to the comfort of those who would rather ignore our pain than to acknowledge that they have been the beneficiaries of our suffering.

The sociology of good cop/bad cop represents different methods of educating the public about what it means to be human in a dehumanizing world. Such an educational environment would better speak to the imagination of the hearer, by which inventive and creative means to resolve the problems of anti-blackness will emerge. Instead of being offended by the anger represented within black protest, the mainstream of America should study the causes and learn to empathize. This attitude would be more in line with the biblical ideal of weeping when others weep and mourning when they mourn. (Romans 12:15.)

Dr. Martin Luther King Jr and Malcolm X were not the first among black heroes and heroines who represented different levels of militancy throughout the history of the struggle. For too many years, those who trafficked in human enslavement made the argument that black people were happy with their plight and are satisfied with their enslaved conditions. This was one of the main comforting self-serving narratives directed at northern abolitionists. Slave insurrections led by Nat Turner, Gabriel Prosser and Denmark Vessey were significant because they counteracted such narratives. Indeed, this created a high level of fear among landowners, particularly in the South, yet had these dramatic events not occurred, the depth of pain they were willing to endure to be free would not have gained the level of attention that was needed. The power of pen and voice by literate Freedmen was powerful and indispensable, but the more extreme measures on behalf of freedom had tremendous value in buttressing the truth that was expressed by those figures.

Bear in mind that Turner, Vessey and Prosser were all Christian preachers, which undermines later rhetoric by black Muslims and socially conscious groups that Christianity has historically made black people docile, manageable and resistant to the ideas of revolution. In fact, Toussant-Louverture, the leader of the successful, yet bloody Haitian Revolution of 1797-1801, was a devout Catholic.[152]

The Haitian Revolution was the greatest uprising among the captives in the Americas. Haiti would become the first independent black state in the Americas in the aftermath of the bloody insurrection. Both the underground revolutions in the US, as well as the slave uprisings had indisputable value to the cause of black freedom and would represent the good cop/bad cop dynamic in American black history. All blacks who yearned for freedom on the mainland, who either heard or read about it, drew inspiration from the Haitian Revolution, according to professor of History, Douglas Egerton of Le Moyne College.[153]

He adds, that it while it gave life and hope to the enslaved, it had the effect of terrorizing Thomas Jefferson and his fellow enslavers.

---

[152] https://www.brown.edu/Facilities/John_Carter_Brown_Library/exhibitions/toussaint/pages/iconography.html

[153] (https://www.pbs.org/wgbh/aia/part3/3i3130.html.)

God would never allow the enslaver to feel comfortable or at ease while participating in the evils of enslavement. Boldly, activist scholar and theological educator at Howard University School of Divinity, Thomas Hoyt Jr., included the fiery black Muslim-Malcolm X, along with other Christian leaders in his version of the hall of heroines and heroes of the faith in the black struggle for freedom. His list included both good cop/bad cops in the national consciousness of White America, but who were all good and righteous in the hearts of black people. Hoyt says in part the following:

Our ancestors were great and powerful people on the continent of Africa. Africa once ruled the world...Our fathers and mothers, sisters and brothers were kidnapped, stolen like cattle from their home in Africa, and brought to America as slaves. They were beaten, molested, and killed...In their suffering they cried out to God and God raised up leaders among them—men and women like Nat Turner, Nathaniel Paul, David Walker, Sojourner Truth, Harriet Tubman, William Miles, Henry McNeal Turner, Marcus Garvey, Malcolm X, Rosa Parks, Martin Luther King Jr., and countless other persons less known but yet of great significance. These men stood up to their oppressors and condemned their inhumanity.[154]

Within this hall of heroes, there are those who attempted to work within the American system of laws, and those who sought revolutionary action. Hoyt clearly states that these all were raised up

---

[154] Hoyt, Thomas. *Stony the Road We Trod, Cain Hope Felder (Ed.), 1991 Minneapolis: Fortress Press, 31*

by God in answer to the cries of the beaten down and molested sufferers. This answer to those cries by raising up such leaders is consistent with the messianic tradition of the biblical Moses. Except for Malcolm X, this hall of heroes is exclusively Christian.

What is significant about Hoyt's inclusion of Malcolm X in his hall of heroes is that he clearly believes that God can and does raise up persons outside of the Christian tradition as he sees fit to achieve his divine purposes for human flourishing and liberation. Hoyt makes the comparison that as Israel, as a community, became liberated from bondage and oppression, God's work in the world is to liberate all people from oppression. Just as the Hebrew bible includes prophets who served contemporaneously for the purpose of liberation and restoration, and operated in distinctively purposeful roles within their era, such as Isaiah and Amos, so did Malcolm X and Dr. Martin Luther King Jr. Such contemporary voices are needed in these times also, because the struggle continues. Malcolm and Martin represent both the socially conscious religion and the historic black church, which are two wings of the same bird seeking for a landing place of survival and flourishing; both wings are a prophetic voice to America and all imperialistic powers.

We believe that God is desperately seeking our salvation. Therefore, prophets will continue to arise both within the church and outside of the church (and in utilizing Paul's theme of warfare) to pull down the strongholds of dehumanizing power, and to cast down white nationalist imaginations, and every high thing [class or racial hierarchy] that exalts itself against the knowledge God has given us about ourselves and bringing every racist political idea to the obedience of Christ (2 Cor. 10:4,5.) This is the essence of black religion wherever it is found.

Works Cited

Arkush, Michael. The Fight of the Century. Hoboken, NJ, John Wiley and Sons, 2008

Atcho, Claude. *Reading Black Books.* Grand Rapids, Michigan, Brazos Press, 2022.

Carmichael, Stokely and Thelwell, Ekweuemene Michael. *Ready for Revolution—The Life and Struggle of Stokely* Carmichael (Kwame Ture.) New York, New York, Shribner, 2003.

Cone, James H. *God of the Oppressed.* Maryknoll, New York, Orbis Books, 1997.

Cone, James H. and Lawrence H. Mamiya. Black Theology and Black Power. Maryknoll, New York, Orbis Books, 2018.

Cone, James H. Malcolm and Martin and America. Maryknoll, New York, Orbis Books, 1991

Curtis, Edward E. *Black Muslim Religion in the Nation of Islam.* Chapel Hill, North Carolina: University Of North Carolina Press, 2006.

Dannin, Robert. *Black Pilgrimage to Islam.* New York: Oxford University Press, 2002.

Douglas, Kelly Brown. *The Black Christ.* New York: Orbis Books, 2019.

Dyson, Michael Eric. *Tears We Cannot Stop.* New York, New York: St. Martin's Press, 2017.

Felder, Cain Hope, (Ed.) Stony the Road We Trod. Minneapolis: Fortress Press, 1991

Haley, Alex. The Autobiography of Malcolm X. New York: Ballentine Books, 1965.

Hopkins, Dwight L. *Introducing Black Theology of Liberation.* Maryknoll, New York, Orbis Books, 2014.

Peniel, Joseph E. *The Sword and the Shield.* New York, Basic Books, 2020.

Lincoln C. Eric, *The Black Church in African American Experience.* Durham, NC, Duke University Press, 1990.

Lincoln, C. Eric. The Black Muslims in America. Third Edition. Grand Rapids Michigan: William B. Eerdmans, 1994.

Malcolm X. "God's Judgment of White America." Press Conference, New York, December 1, 1963.

Malcolm X, Speech on Police Brutality Surrounding Ronald Stokes. Los Angeles, California, May 20, 1962.

Malcolm X, Interview following the conversion of Cassius Clay to Muhammad Ali Lewis Lomax, New York, February 1, 1964.

Mallory, Tamika, Speech at Press Conference about George Floyd Police Murder. Minneapolis, MN, May 29, 2020.

Manis, Andrew. A Fire You Can't Put Out--The Civil Rights Life of Birmingham's Reverend Fred Shuttlesworth. Tuscaloosa, Alabama: University Of Alabama Press, 1999.

Mason, Eric (General Editor.) *Urban Apologetics-Restoring Black Dignity with the Gospel.* Grand Rapids MI, Zondervan, 2021.

Martin Luther King Jr., Drum Major Instinct Sermon. Ebenezer Baptist Church, Atlanta Georgia, February 4, 1968.
McCaulley, Esau. Reading While Black. Westmont, Illinois, Intervarsity Press, 2020.

Nelson, Hart M.; Anne Kusener Nelson (1975). Black Church in the 1960s. Lexington, KY. University Press of Kentucky, 2014.

Onaci, Edward. *Free the Land: The Republic of New Afrika and the Pursuit of a Black Nation State.* Chapel Hill, North Carolina. UNC Press Books, 2020.

Roberts, Deotis J. *Liberation and Reconciliation.* Maryknoll NY, Orbis Books, 1994.

Soulen, R. Kendall and Woodhead, Linda. *God and Human Dignity.* Grand Rapids MI. Wm. B. Eerdmans. 2006

Speller, Julia Michelle. Unashamedly Black and unapologetically Christian: One congregation's quest for meaning and belonging (PhD thesis). The University of Chicago. p. 2005

Turner, Richard Brent. Islam in the African American Experience. Indianapolis: Indiana University Press, 1997.

Warnock, Raphael. Divided Mind of the Black Church. New York, NYU Press, 2013.

White, Vibert L. Inside the Nation of Islam: A Historical Personal Testimony of a Black Muslim. Gainesville: University Press of Florida, 2001.

Online Resources

https://noi.org/muslim-program/

https://www.blackpast.org/african-american-history/2008-rev-jeremiah-wright-confusing-god-and-government/

https://muslimadvocates.org/police-violence-statement/

https://www.cleveland.com/pdextra/2012/01/martin_luther_king_jr_april_26.html

https://goblackcentral.com/2013/01/the-martin-luther-king-you-rarely-hear/

https://www.gphistorical.org/mlk/mlkspeech/#:~:text=And%20I%20must%20say%20tonight,justice%20have%20not%20been%20met.

https://www.c-span.org/video/?318826-1/1963-interview-malcolm

https://www.brown.edu/Facilities/John_Carter_Brown_Library/exhibitions/toussaint/pages/iconography.html

https://www.pbs.org/wgbh/aia/part3/3i3130.html (Thomas Egerton, Le Moyne College, PBS Interview)

https://www.theguardian.com/books/2023/may/10/martin-luther-king-jonathan-eig-book-malcolm-x

https://genius.com/Nas-i-can-lyrics

https://kinginstitute.stanford.edu/encyclopedia/ghana-trip

https://prospect.org/civil-rights/malcolm-x-and-martin-luther-king-jr-shake-hands/

https://www.whitehouse.gov/briefing-room/speeches-remarks/2023/02/07/remarks-of-president-joe-biden-state-of-the-union-address-as-prepared-for-delivery/

https://twitter.com/BreeNewsome/status/1618991962497097730

https://sojo.net/magazine/february-2019/advocate-benjamin-crump-faith-christian

"God is a Negro: The (rhetorical) black theology of bishop Henry McNeal" by Andre E. Johnson (memphis.edu)

https://www.encyclopedia.com/people/history/us-history-biographies/henry-mcneal-turner